ROUTLEDGE LIBRARY EDITIONS: EDUCATION

SOCIETY AND THE TEACHER'S ROLE

SOCIETY AND THE TEACHER'S ROLE

FRANK MUSGROVE AND
PHILIP H. TAYLOR

Volume 228

LONDON AND NEW YORK

First published in 1969

This edition first published in 2012
by Routledge
2 Park Square, Milton Park, Abingdon, Oxfordshire OX14 4RN

Simultaneously published in the USA and Canada
by Routledge
711 Third Avenue, New York, NY 10017

First issued in paperback 2014

Routledge is an imprint of the Taylor & Francis Group, an informa business

© 1969 Frank Musgrove and Philip H. Taylor

All rights reserved. No part of this book may be reprinted or reproduced or utilised in any form or by any electronic, mechanical, or other means, now known or hereafter invented, including photocopying and recording, or in any information storage or retrieval system, without permission in writing from the publishers.

Trademark notice: Product or corporate names may be trademarks or registered trademarks, and are used only for identification and explanation without intent to infringe.

British Library Cataloguing in Publication Data
A catalogue record for this book is available from the British Library

ISBN13: 978-0-415-69891-7 (Volume 228)
ISBN13: 978-1-138-00760-4 (pbk)

Publisher's Note
The publisher has gone to great lengths to ensure the quality of this reprint but points out that some imperfections in the original copies may be apparent.

Disclaimer
The publisher has made every effort to trace copyright holders and would welcome correspondence from those they have been unable to trace.

Society and the Teacher's Role

FRANK MUSGROVE

PHILIP H. TAYLOR

LONDON
ROUTLEDGE & KEGAN PAUL

*First published in 1969
by Routledge & Kegan Paul Limited
Broadway House, 68–74 Carter Lane
London EC4V 5EL*

Reprinted 1971

*Printed in Great Britain by
Lowe & Brydone (Printers) Ltd., London
© Frank Musgrove & Philip H. Taylor, 1969
No part of this book may be reproduced
in any form without permission from
the publisher, except for the quotation
of brief passages in criticism*

ISBN 0 7100 7225 2 (p)
ISBN 0 7100 6447 0 (c)

Contents

1	The Teacher and Society	1
2	The Expectations of Pupils	17
3	The Expectations of Parents	28
4	Teachers' Role Conflicts	43
5	Parents versus Teachers	58
6	Problems of Status and Role	68
7	Teachers and Clients	79
	Appendix. The Provision of Private Education in the Nineteenth Century	90
	Notes	91
	Index	101

Tables

		page
1.	Weight Attached by Children to Three Areas of Teacher Behaviour	24
2.	Weight Attached by Teachers to Three Areas of Teacher Behaviour	25
3.	Subjects' Social Status	30
4.	Age of Subjects	30
5.	Emphasis on Responsibility of School or Home	32
6.	Parents' Claims to Direct Behaviour	33
7.	Parents' Secondary School Preferences	37
8.	Reasons for Preferring the Grammar School	38
9.	Domestic Science Teachers' Evaluation of Personality	50
10.	Male Grammar School Teachers' Perceived Expectations of Others	52
11.	Female Grammar School Teachers' Perceived Expectations of Others	52
12.	Male Secondary Modern School Teachers' Perceived Expectations of Others	52
13.	Female Secondary Modern School Teachers' Perceived Expectations of Others	53
14.	Role Conflict and Social Area (Junior School Teachers)	55
15.	Role Conflict and Social Area (Infant School Teachers)	55
16.	Restricted or Diffuse Role Conception of Junior and Infant School Teachers According to Sex and Marital Status	62
17.	Teachers' Restricted or Diffuse Role Conception According to Social-Class Area and Denominational Status of School	62
18.	Ascription of Diffuse or Restricted Role to Teachers by Parents	63

	page
19. Median Rank Order of Teachers' Aims	64
20. Prestige Ranking of Teachers	75
21. Function of Teachers as Seen by 116 Teachers	76
22. Rank and Function	77

Figures

	page
1. Teacher Attributes Ranked by Subjects for Self and Others	47
2. Teacher-Emphasis, Perceived Headteacher and Pupil-Emphasis on 'Discipline' and 'Personality' (Men Teachers)	51
3. Teacher-Emphasis, Perceived Headteacher and Pupil-Emphasis on 'Discipline' and 'Personality' (Women Teachers)	57
4. Teacher-Evaluation, Perceived Parent-Evaluation, and Actual Parent-Evaluation	65

Acknowledgements

Four chapters of this book are based on inquiries which the authors have published in research journals. They thank the editor of the *British Journal of Educational Psychology* for permission to use previously published material in chapters two and five, of the *Sociological Review* for permission to use previously published material in chapter three, and of *Educational Sciences* for permission to use previously published research in chapter four.

Chapter One
THE TEACHER AND SOCIETY

THE RISE OF A NEW DESPOTISM

During the past hundred years there has grown up in our midst a new despotism: the rule of the teachers. Today they claim to decide what kind of people we shall be. This is not a joint and generally agreed decision even among the teachers themselves. One school has decided that Englishmen shall be decorous and self-restrained; another that they shall show greater spontaneity, even gaiety; a third that they shall be rooted in the ancient values of their locality; a fourth that they shall have broad horizons, that they shall be 'universal men'. Curriculum, teaching methods and school organization are shaped to achieve these ends. In order that these, and a thousand others, shall be pursued with all the resources of pedagogic art, it is sufficient that the teachers have decided upon their course.

Even within a given school one teacher may be organizing his work and modifying his methods to produce Englishmen who approximate to the Pueblo Indians: encouraging co-operation and discouraging competition, using group methods, placing stress on creativity, he aims to produce human beings who place the common good above individual reputation. Next door his colleague aims to produce Englishmen who approximate to the Comanches: courageous, individualistic, enterprising, full of dash and initiative. For him mark lists and orders of merit are important instruments of policy; individual work is encouraged; punishment is inflicted to breed stoicism rather than to effect reformation. It is conceivable that the parents of these children want neither Pueblos or Comanches. This is an irrelevance. Only if the children are patently being trained to be neo-Nazis or polygynists would protest be likely or even seem in order.

A school will decide in a hundred ways what kind of human beings to produce: when it decides to run a Scout troop rather

Society and the Teacher's Role

than a Combined Cadet Force; to stream or to de-stream; to teach Chinese and Persian or commercial French; to enforce or to abolish school uniform; to have prefects elected or nominated; to let boys sit with girls. These vital decisions – and a thousand others – will be made by the teachers themselves; they need the ratification of no higher authority; they are, in the strict sense, irresponsible. Only those parents who are rich enough to buy their children out of the maintained schools are able to decide, in some measure, what their children shall become.

The new despotism is a century old. It dates, at least in the grammar schools, from the eighteen-sixties. The groundwork for this licence was laid by the Taunton Commission. (In the elementary schools it was delayed by more than a quarter of a century by the Revised Elementary Code and the system of payment-by-results which effectively prescribed the teacher's role. Only the work of the National Union of Elementary Teachers secured for teachers at this level the licence enjoyed by schools at the secondary stage.)

Before the *Report of the Schools Inquiry (Taunton) Commission* in 1868 – and particularly before the Grammar Schools Act of 1840 – sovereignty in educational affairs resided neither with teachers nor parents, but with the law. The charter of the endowed schools was the legal instrument which defined the teacher's role. Sometimes it was possible to re-interpret the charter or to circumvent it. (The great Victorian headmasters like Arnold and Kennedy had the cunning and ruthlessness to evade their legal responsibilities, though they commonly spent a great deal of time and the wealth of the foundation in prolonged litigation.) In general the law remained inflexible, upheld to the letter by the courts as in the celebrated judgment of Lord Eldon in 1805 concerning the curriculum of Leeds Grammar School. The law could not easily be trifled with and neither parents nor teachers could flout the founder's intention of what should be taught and even how to teach it.

The obligations of schoolmasters both in their general behaviour and the practice of their art were commonly very closely defined. At Oundle 'Neither the master nor the usher shall be common gamesters, haunters of taverns, neither to exceed in apparel nor any other ways to be an infamy to the school or give evil example to the scholars to whom in all points they ought to show themselves examples of honest, continent and godly behaviour'. At Chigwell Grammar School in Essex the second master must be 'a man skilful in Greek and Latin tongues, a good poet, of sound religion, neither Papist nor Puritan, of a grave behaviour, of a sober and honest conversation, no tipler or haunter of alehouses, no puffer of tobacco . . .' The curriculum was usually specified in the same detail as the schoolmaster's qualifications and deportment, even the books which the scholars were to use.

But there was a comparatively easy escape from the tyranny of the law: parents who were rich enough could establish or promote new foundations which conducted themselves and taught subjects as they decreed. The early and mid-nineteenth century was the heyday of the (middle-class) parent for whom a multitude of private and proprietary schools sprang into existence. Even the trustees of grammar schools, powerless to change the legal restrictions imposed by the foundation, opened rival (private) schools in the neighbourhood and guaranteed them a minimum number of pupils. In some cases they even persuaded the schoolmaster to leave the grammar school for the private establishment, exchanging the sovereignty of the law for the sovereignty of parents.[1]

In the eighteen-sixties there were some 37,000 boys in 542 ancient endowed grammar schools and 30 new endowed grammar schools; some 12,000 boys in 86 new proprietary schools, and probably at least another 40,000 in private schools – excluding the new preparatory schools, which probably contained 7,000 boys. The private schools offered the services which parents defined; the schoolmaster gave proper attention to his clients' will. He could not flout it by referring to the legal requirements of a charter (though he learned to protect himself behind the regulations of the new public examinations like the Oxford and Cambridge 'Locals'); he had not yet learned to claim a supreme authority *qua* teacher.

The new proprietary and private schools promised to inculcate the values and teach the skills and knowledge of which parents approved. Parents who were Roman Catholics, Anglicans, Quakers, Wesleyan Methodists, Primitive Methodists, or Congregationalists, supported new schools which would mould human beings to their specifications. They were not prepared to accept the specifications of any other authority. New private and proprietary schools which tried to dictate their own terms went out of business, as a report from Yorkshire made clear to the Taunton Commission: 'All the schools which have been established by joint-stock companies, for the promotion of general education, have proved to be financial failures. The only proprietary schools which have succeeded are those founded by religious bodies for the education of their own children.'[2] (For further details of the provision of private education in the nineteenth century, see Appendix.)

The Taunton Commission could see no virtue in schools which submitted to parental influence. The great expansion of Victorian private schools suffered from this defect: clients defined the services they required. Although the clients came predominantly from the professional and mercantile classes, their judgment in regard to the education of their own children was not to be trusted: they were so misguided as to want 'modern' subjects, even a vocational bias in the curriculum; they had no appreciation of the disciplined mind produced by the Classics:

> Now it is quite certain, that it cannot be said, that the majority of parents of the middle classes are really good judges of education . . . of the best means of training the mind, and of strengthening the faculties, they are no judges at all.[3]

The Taunton Commission referred to middle-class parents with the same tremendous condescension that Mathew Arnold spoke during this period of the 'Philistines' in his *Culture and Anarchy*. They could not be trusted to place sufficient emphasis on 'the cultivation of the understanding, on the refinement of the thoughts and manners, on what is solid and permanent, rather than on what is showy and transitory . . .'[4] Vital decisions about their own children could be made only by the *literati*, the elect who had been vouchsafed sweetness and light.

It would be absurd to pretend that all, or even most, of the private schools which middle-class parents were supporting in the middle of the century were everything that could be desired. Many were ephemeral, inefficient, inadequately staffed.[5] But many private schoolmasters were convinced from the start that the Commission did not approach them with an open mind. As Mr. Stanton reported from the South-West: 'There was undoubtedly a general impression prevailing among the masters [in private schools] that the inquiry was hostile to their interests. The names of some of the Commissioners were quoted as taking a hostile view....'[6]

The general verdict of the Taunton Commission in respect of private schools has been accepted at its face value for too long. In passing final judgment on all the evidence they had assembled, even the Commissioners were forced grudgingly to concede that many private schools were not simply good, but of outstanding quality: they specialized in individual tuition, they were flexible in their curricula and organization; they were pioneering advances in educational practices and techniques.[7]

But these schools were subject to the pressures of parents, and these pressures were invariably 'in the direction of some special training for an occupation in after life'.[8] The endowed schools were protected against their clients, and parents often preferred private schools because 'they do not like the high and independent line which is taken by a fairly well endowed public school'.[9] The Commission was outraged by the report of Mr. Fitch from Yorkshire that in some larger private schools, it seemed, 'each parent had made a separate contract as to the amount of comfort and attention his child should receive'.[10]

Mr. Assistant Commissioner Stanton spoke with approval of the headmaster who 'has no committee to consult for any change he may think requisite. He is a despot within his own limits. To an able man this is an advantage, and all our greatest schoolmasters have been those who have been least interfered with.'[11]

This was the ideal of the Taunton Commission: the maximum freedom for schoolmasters, the minimum for parents. The latter should have representation on the governing boards of grammar schools, but they should be counterbalanced by other governors 'appointed on the grounds of their larger knowledge, and to represent education generally'.[12] To the headmaster 'should be assigned all the internal discipline, the choice of books and methods; the organization, and the appointment and dismissal of assistants'.[13] And 'In the internal management as a general rule the less the trustees interfere in the matter the better'.[14]

In the last two decades of the century Charlotte Mason attempted to rally parents against the new power of the schoolmaster. She rebuked (middle-class) parents for their 'abdication',[15] and attempted to organize them for effective association in their children's education. The Parents' National Educational Union (1887) and the 'House of Education' (1892) at Ambleside were a recognition of the dethronement of parents and an attempt to secure parental reinstatement.

During the last quarter of the nineteenth century there was one sphere of education (outside the independent schools) in which parents were extremely influential and secured an education for their children which accorded closely with their wishes – in the higher grade schools maintained under the Elementary Code by the larger urban school boards. The boards of the larger cities (established under the Education Act of 1870) were under strong pressure particularly from lower middle-class parents to establish schools with curricula relevant to an industrial and commercial nation.

In 1895 there were three higher grade schools in London and 60 elsewhere in England, mainly in the industrial North and Midlands.[16] The demand in London came largely from people 'with incomes from £150 to £200 a year';[17] in Leeds 'persons of good social position, enjoying large incomes', were sending their children to the higher grade school.[18] At Sheffield, while the grammar school had 160 pupils, there were 1,000 in the higher grade school 'who turn their superior knowledge to good practical account in the manufactures. A very considerable proportion of the boys really go to useful careers in the large works.'[19]

The growth of such schools with a technical and commercial bias was the result of parental pressures. As the vice-chairman of the Birmingham School Board explained to the Bryce Commission:

> The demand for these board secondary schools . . . has increased year by year in volume and intensity in the large urban centres of population; and the pressure to meet this demand has been so great upon the schools boards, and the reasonableness of the demand so obvious, that all the boards of the larger provincial towns – Liverpool, Manchester, Birmingham, Leeds, Sheffield, and others – have been forced into making efforts to supply the kind of school demanded.[20]

The famous Cockerton Judgment of 1899[21] was an affront to parents as much as a blow to the school boards which had responded so sensitively to their needs. The nineteenth century

The Teacher and Society

ended with the virtual exclusion of clients from any direct influence in publicly financed education. (The direct link – and power – which the payment of fees afforded finally disappeared after World War II.) The new and remoter local education authorities established under the Act of 1902 were a buffer rather than a link between school and client.[22]

This was felt to be the case particularly perhaps in rural areas. George Bourne has described the sense of exclusion of country people:

> In the education of their children, for one thing, they [the people] have no voice at all. It is administered in a standardized form by a committee of middle-class people appointed in the neighbouring town, who carry out provisions which originate from unapproachable permanent officials in Whitehall. The County Council may modify the programme a little; His Majesty's Inspectors – strangers to the people, and ignorant of their needs – issue fiats in the form of advice to the school teachers; and meanwhile the parents of the children acquiesce, not always approving what is done, but accepting it as if it were a law of fate that all such things must be arranged over their heads by the classes who have book-learning.[23]

By the end of the nineteenth century teachers in maintained schools had escaped the constrictions of the law and the direct pressures of their clients. The new authorities which have since employed them have not sought to impose similar constraints. Teachers were set free. The Board of Education, the Ministry of Education, the local authorities, and the governing bodies of schools have been notable for their self-restraint.[24] They have provided only the broad administrative framework within which the teacher does his job.

While Her Majesty's Inspectors have been reluctant to surrender their name, local authority inspectors have commonly been restyled advisers. The President of the Board of Education had only rather ill-defined powers of 'superintendence'; the Butler Act of 1944 gave the Minister the right to assume more positive functions.[25] A more positive approach has been taken only with the greatest caution. The consequent freedom of teachers is the profession's glory; it is the people's shame.

The new Certificate of Secondary Education has gone to

remarkable lengths to escape the charge of directing teachers what to teach and how to teach it. *Examinations Bulletin No. 1* affirms that the content of syllabuses, the nature and the marking of examination papers, must be firmly in the teachers' hands.[26] Although the *Bulletin* points out that parents, commerce, industry, local authorities and other agencies have a contribution to make to discussions about curriculum, teaching methods and examinations, it accepts 'the teachers' final responsibility for curricular decisions'.[27]

SHAPING THE CONTEMPORARY TEACHER'S ROLE

The teacher's role in mid-twentieth-century England is determined by a variety of informal (and often conflicting) forces, pressures and expectations, often difficult to define or trace to their source. It cannot be described by reference to a legal charter, to a contract with clients, or even to the detailed prescription of employers. An examination of some of these informal pressures and expectations, which today are so important, is the central concern of this book.

The role of the teacher in modern society has proved an inexhaustible subject for arm-chair theorizing and inaugural lectures. There are virtually no empirical studies of the contemporary role of teachers, at least in Britain. This book is an attempt to provide, on a very limited scale, some empirical data on teachers' conceptions of their function today and the complex of expectations within which they operate. It is primarily concerned to offer a factual picture; but some reflections are offered in conclusion on the changes which should occur in the function of the teacher in a changing democratic society.

This book reports studies of the way teachers see their job, the way they think that other people significantly related to their work see it, and the way these people (particularly parents and pupils) do in fact see it. It is a study of conflict, of the often contrary demands which are made upon teachers or which they feel are made upon them. For the very freedom which teachers enjoy creates uncertainties: they work in an ill-defined situation.[28] We offer only a small-scale attempt to plot something of the field of tension and uncertainty in which teachers of our day appear to find themselves.

The Teacher and Society

Today the teacher arrives at a conception of his proper or necessary role through his own experience as a pupil, his experience at the job, his reading, exchange of views, and reflection – and, of course, his professional training. 'The Principles of Education' still figure prominently in the training course: an unrigorous 'philosophy' of education, a miscellany of ideas about the aims of education in the light of which, it is at least implied and probably explicitly stated, he must arrive at his own notion of what his job entails and the aims he must pursue.

But probably the most important influence for many teachers is the staff room, the group of colleagues which he joins, with whom he must live and work, whose respect he must earn. (Those who inhabit annexes for woodwork, domestic science, art, etc., may feel fewer constraints but suffer more anxiety. There is urgent need for research into the influence of school architecture on the morale and role difficulties of teachers.)

The teacher will usually learn to conform to the values and practices of his colleagues; they will fortify him in his resistance to the perhaps divergent notions of headmasters, H.M.I.s, local authority advisers, parents, and the boys and girls he teaches. All these may, with varying force and varying methods, put to him notions of how he should do this job, what he should be aiming at. Thus he may be torn between the contrary demands of pupils and headteacher, standing as a bridge between their opposed expectations, seeing the former as demanding of sympathy and understanding, the latter comparatively indifferent to the exercise of these qualities: his own evaluation of the importance of these qualities falls somewhere in between; he is located at the point of maximum tension. (See below, Chapter four.) His capacity to tolerate such cross-pressures will be increased if he stands four-square with twenty or thirty men in the same predicament. The staff room is probably one of the most potent forces for conservatism in English education.

The individuals, organizations and authorities which help to shape the teacher's role, to push him this way or that, vary with the type of school and the locality in which it is situated. The local community, through its official or unofficial leaders, can still make heavy demands particularly perhaps on junior schools, influencing their objectives, calling on the teachers – particularly headteachers – for a wide range of services outside the classroom and the school in so-called 'voluntary' work particularly with the youth of the district. For some, flight through change of job or residence is the only answer to an intolerable situation; yet local education authorities may strongly urge their head and assistant teachers to live in the community even when school houses are not provided.

If the community which the junior school serves is geographically isolated, or if it serves a well-to-do middle-class area, parents may still bear quite heavily on the teachers. In the former case they may expect from them a wide range of burdensome social work; in the latter (as we show in Chapter three) they will make heavy demands to have an academic syllabus rigorously followed. Parents will have views on 'streaming', on teaching methods, on the content of the curriculum; and they will be sufficiently articulate and socially assured to confront the teacher and make their views known. Mother and father may constitute a formidable joint-force on Parents' Evening. (By contrast working-class parents will be less forbidding; mother is less likely to be supported by father on her visits to the school; and her appearance there, especially uninvited, is likely to be far less frequent. One should beware of concluding from this that they are less interested; they are less socially assured.)

The influence of clients will also vary with the voluntariness and the selectivity of the educational institutions which serve them. If a school or college is open to anyone who wishes to attend, like many courses in adult and further education, the wishes of students (and perhaps of employers or parents who have sent them on the course) will carry considerable weight. Students will have their own views of the proper objectives of the curriculum, and lecturers and college authorities will be unwise to ignore them. But clients are comparatively powerless when institutions can require compulsory attendance and at the same time be highly selective in their intake. The English grammar school is a good example of this second position.

The power of clients in an American voluntary, unselective institution has been described by Burton Clark in his book, *The Open Door College*. The two-year junior college meets the increased demand for post-high school education in America and is open to all who wish to attend. Clark points out that 'Selection is a control device. . . . Such control is evident in private colleges,

The Teacher and Society

which selectively cultivate a social base and structure their clientele.' This control device is lacking in the open-door college. 'With nonselection comes a weakening of control and enlarging of the discretion of potential students.'

Clark shows how in the open-door college the student's 'voluntariness becomes an active force. He can decide for himself whether and when he will enter and actively contend for his own version of the ends and means of his education. The conjunction of nonselection and age above compulsory schooling in the public junior college gives maximum thrust to the choices and characteristics of students.' 'Of all types of school the unselective-voluntary type will be most open to wide clientele influence.' In more sociological terms: 'The public junior college is at the point in the educational structure where professional dictation is likely to be minimal.'[29]

The only way to thwart the will of clients is through 'counselling'. The open-door college devotes much time and attention to this activity. In the college which Clark investigated, 80 per cent of the staff considered that counselling was as important or more important than instruction. The counsellor persuades the student to accept a type of education (and a type of career after its conclusion) which he was not at first disposed to accept. This process of thwarting the client's will is more picturesquely referred to as 'cooling him out'. The spread of counselling in our schools is one of the most potentially sinister features of the contemporary educational scene. It can become a device for restoring a teacher despotism which other forces have eroded. As more children of limited ability stay on in English schools beyond the statutory leaving age, we can expect to see an army of counsellors employed to cool them out.

But in general, in English education today, what is still remarkable is not the power of clients (whether pupils or their parents), but their impotence. The twentieth century has been remarkable for the exclusion of parents from direct contact with teachers and schools. Partly, the parents have abdicated; but probably more important, the teachers have skilfully protected themselves from 'interference'. The Parent-Teacher Association movement has been to all intents and purposes stillborn.

This is not surprising. The teachers never intended that parents should actually exercise power – over anything that mattered.

They could meet the mentors of their children in order to hear what was being done, perhaps to give material aid for doing more, and to ratify what the teachers had in any case decided. It is unlikely that parents anywhere will continue indefinitely to attend on such terms. The strikingly different vitality of the American P.T.A. is quite simply explained: it has authority.

Parental 'interference' in the curriculum, teaching methods, staff appointments (and dismissals) is unthinkable to teachers in English maintained schools. But parental influence may nevertheless be felt – if only to be ridiculed, scorned and rejected. There are social class as well as area differences in this matter. It seems probable from the inquiries reported below (Chapter three) that at the junior school stage middle-class parents make a less extensive range of demands on the school than working-class parents do (or would wish to do): they feel that they can cope, that they can themselves do much for the child in the way of social and moral training and even formal academic instruction.

The working-class parent is less certain; and perhaps less well equipped to do so. She looks to the school to help her child 'get on' in life; and, in a 'poor' area, may feel that the school alone can effectively protect the child from the undesirable social influences which surround it. At the secondary stage the demands are reversed: the middle-class parent makes heavy demands to provide the training which ensures a successful middle-class career; the working-class parent has assumed that the child can now, in any case, take care of itself and provide for the future.

Among the most powerful influences which have modified the teacher's role in recent years are the theories of the sociologists and psychologists. These theories are mediated by professional training and to some extent by the inspectorate; they are by no means wholly accepted. But current views about the importance of groups in education, on the one hand, and the need for love and affection in dealing with the young, on the other, have doubtless been potent influences on the teacher's view of his job. To the extent that he has accepted them he has probably alienated himself from his pupils, who still, in the main, see his job essentially as teaching, i.e. instructing and explaining. (See Chapter two.) He may see himself primarily as a dispenser of sympathy and understanding; or as a peer-group facilitator and mediator.

'The ultimate educational unit is never the individual but the group', maintained Mannheim.[30] Piaget has argued that logical thinking and even a rational morality derive from group interaction.[31] John Locke's belief that the child could learn nothing from other children but vice, appeared to have been exploded; indeed, discipline and morality were not conditions imposed from without and above by adult authority, but by-products of peer-group life. The teacher's job was to let this life in groups achieve all that it was capable of achieving; Riesman had distinguished the peer-group as the real teacher in an 'other-directed' society.[32]

If formerly the child could learn nothing from his coevals but vice, now he could learn little of value from anybody else. The nominal teacher must efface himself; he must create the conditions in which learning can take place; he becomes a stage-manager; but the posturing – and in particular the soliloquies – of the actor are out. The Dalton Plan and its modifications enabled him to abdicate his traditional role without actually causing chaos. He became a chief clerk. Dewey sanctioned his renunciation of words in favour of pupil activity. The teacher who spoke to his class, as a class, for more than five consecutive minutes must be crushed by a load of guilt for failing to conform to the new role assigned to him by philosophers, sociologists and psychologists. In his initial training, no matter how vital, stimulating and informative his talking might be, it would earn him the censure of his supervisor for 'lecturing' rather than 'teaching'. The prime requisite of the new teacher is that he shall not teach.

Over-emphasized and unrealistically applied theories of child development have similarly removed the emphasis in teaching from intellectual exchange to social relationship. Experience of the job, the pressure from pupils (and colleagues) to be effective as well as kind (or even to be effective instead of kind), no doubt helps to change in some measure the values inculcated in teacher training.[33] But whatever doubts and conflicts there are among trainers of teachers today – and there is evidence of confusion of a high order in their theories and practices – they appear to be unanimous in the importance they attach to sympathetic understanding of children and to establishing a happy and harmonious relationship with pupils inside (and if possible outside) the classroom.

In an inquiry into the aims of supervisors of graduate student teachers in the University of London, little agreement was found regarding 'the attributes which contribute to success in teaching practice'. Fifty major attributes of the successful student teacher were put forward by supervisors: this wide range of qualities included such diverse accomplishments as 'Ability to organize', 'Good appearance', 'Extraversion', 'Sincerity', and 'Punctuality and regularity of attendance'. When the supervisors rated the importance of these attributes, there was general agreement only in the prime importance attached to the group of characteristics embraced by 'Attitude and insight in dealing with others'. Out of eight main clusters of attributes which were isolated, this was ranked first. 'Teaching abilities' (including the ability to promote interest) ranked third. 'Practical abilities in teaching' (including the ability to organize a lesson effectively) ranked seventh.[34]

Children appreciate kindness and sympathetic understanding; they also appreciate the opportunity to exercise their intellect and imagination. They perceive the school as an institution specially designed for this purpose. They feel thwarted if all they receive there is kindly personal relationships with adults. The family is the institution which has today specialized in affection; and the child will feel equally thwarted if he fails to find kindness there, and is offered instruction instead. Children and young people demand mainly 'expressive' satisfactions of their homes, 'instrumental' satisfactions of their schools.[35] At school children expect to be taught, to have mysteries explained. For them the good teacher is someone with something to say and clarity in saying it. In spite of their training and the sociological and psychological theories which nowadays pervade the schools, teachers in general seem to perceive the importance of this demand and to agree with it.

The teacher-role is not simply the product of external pressures and expectations, an automatic result of social circumstances. Teachers have a large say in its content and design. They resist some pressures, they accept others; they resist or respond to some which are not in fact there, but are no less real as psychological facts. Our research shows teachers singularly united in rejecting the role which Wilson has ascribed to them as 'social selectors',[36] inculcators and assessors of skills, knowledge, attitudes and values appropriate to 'getting on'. While they believe this to be a prime expectation of parents, whether they teach in secondary modern

The Teacher and Society

or in grammar schools they reject it as any part of their business. As a matter of social fact it is inescapably their business; as a matter of psychological fact it has no part in their remarkably idealistic self-image, it makes no contribution to their motivation except, perhaps, negatively, as something to abjure.

The conflict between social realities and an idealized view of their function is supported in some measure by bogus history, by reference to a golden age of teaching which in fact never existed. In the Golden Age learning was pursued for its own sake; parents faithfully carried out their full parental role (care of the child's health, morals and social development), teachers were free to attend to their proper pedagogical duties. The pressures towards the extension of the teacher's role, particularly to embrace what are seen as properly parental duties, are widely resisted. It is possible that these pressures come less from parents than from sociologists; but the working mother is discussed at morning break in staff rooms throughout the land as the root of many teachers' problems and pupils' deficiencies: she is seen as the extreme case of the abdicating parent. There is no evidence whatsoever in extensive research that the working mother presents teachers with children who are more difficult and demanding (though they may be more resourceful) than the non-working mother. But the teacher feels that he must be protected from her.

It is a mistake, then, to see the teacher's role today as the sum or resultant of external social pressures and demands. His own role-conception, derived from a variety of sources, is surprisingly resilient. It may persist in spite of its incongruence with the social realities of a changing world. New social conditions, new institutions, new types of school, may take a surprisingly long time to modify the teacher's view of his function. The secondary modern school may arise on the grave of the old elementary school, but amidst the uncertainties about its aims old values may persist. 'The good teacher' may still be seen by his superiors, and by his colleagues, as the man who first and foremost – as in the long past days of payment-by-results – is accurate, meticulous, neat and punctual in his completion of the register. The grammar school teacher demonstrates his superiority (as well as by styling himself schoolmaster) by his cavalier disregard of registers or their perfunctory completion if he is obliged to keep them.

If the role of the teacher is due for redefinition, it should be made in the light of established fact about the possibilities and impossibilities of educational procedures and provisions. What *can* the teacher do for individuals, for social groups, for nations? What is the return, in terms of personality development or of economic growth, from particular forms of educational practice? We do not know, because we have not so far attempted systematically to find out. In the meantime the teacher is under pressure to achieve a variety of incompatible impossibilities. He must ensure the nation's uninterrupted economic and technological advance; he must eradicate delinquency and provide a substitute or prop for family life; he must destroy, or at least considerably attenuate, the link between child and home in the interests of social mobility and social justice. The teacher's freedom is also his dilemma. This book attempts to delineate from empirical research something of the nature and magnitude of this conflict.

Chapter Two
THE EXPECTATIONS OF PUPILS

Pupils expect teachers to teach. They value lucid exposition, the clear statement of problems and guidance in their solution. Personal qualities of kindness, sympathy and patience are secondary, appreciated by pupils if they make the teacher more effective in carrying out his primary, intellectual task. At least in our day schools, there appears to be little demand by pupils that teachers shall be friends or temporary mothers and fathers. They are expected to assume an essentially intellectual and instrumental role.

This appears to be broadly true for all stages of education from the infants' school to the university. Enquiries carried out in England and America over half a century have pointed to this conclusion. At the end of the nineteenth century Kratz reported an investigation which showed that schoolchildren demanded first and foremost of their teachers 'help in study'.[1] In the nineteen-thirties Hollis conducted research with over 8,000 children of different ages in both mixed and single-sex schools: the characteristic of teachers which they valued most highly was the ability to explain difficulties patiently. Other teacher characteristics in descending order of importance were: sympathy; fairness; humour; readiness to accept children's questions; wide interests; firm discipline.[2]

In a study of the expectations of the older adolescent pupil in America, Michael found that the teacher's method of teaching was judged to be his most important attribute. Of less importance were the teacher's 'personality' and his mode of enforcing discipline.[3] These findings are in line with research carried out by Allen in English secondary modern schools. Both boys and girls were found to value most highly the teacher's competence as an instructor, his pedagogical skills. But they also wanted their teachers to make lessons interesting, to take a joke, and to be friendly and approachable.[4]

Comparatively little work has been done on the expectations of university students, but one study of English science undergraduates indicates that they demand first and foremost of a lecturer that he 'presents his material clearly and logically'. The students who took part in this inquiry rated forty lecturer characteristics. At the top of the list were: 'Enables the student to understand the basic principles of the subject' and 'Makes his material intelligibly meaningful'. Far less weight was attached to a lecturer's more 'human' characteristics: 'Has a sympathetic attitude towards students' came thirty-second in order of importance, 'Is spontaneous and friendly' came thirty-fourth, and 'Appears to enjoy teaching' came thirty-sixth.[5]

More indirect approaches to the study of pupils' expectations have produced similar results. American high school pupils have been asked to say which of their classes they have found especially good, satisfying and worthwhile, and then to describe what went on in these classes, what they got out of them, and what they found enjoyable. First in importance was subject matter, second the type of classroom activity that the lesson required, and third the teacher's pedagogical ability. Far less weight was attached to the teacher's personal and social qualities: only 9 per cent of the pupils' responses referred to these, while 27 per cent referred to subject matter. 'Evidently, high school juniors do attribute their plus and minus experiences to more than the personal and social variables of their teachers.'[6]

There is little evidence that pupils are expecting their teachers to take on a less specialized role with reduced emphasis on pedagogical functions. Home rather than school is still the main source of expressive, emotional satisfactions. The school and its teachers are expected to meet instrumental (mainly intellectual) needs. A study of adolescents' demands of home and school in England has shown this sharp contrast in expectations. When young people between 14 and 18 years of age were asked what they expected of their homes, 77 per cent of their statements referred to 'expressive' needs: feeling wanted, secure, appreciated and the like. Approximately 50 per cent of the statements about school were in expressive terms. Thirteen categories of demand were distinguished (6 'instrumental' and 7 'expressive'). By far the greatest demand of school fell in the 'intellectual' category. Approximately a quarter of all the statements about school referred to the need for intellectual activity and achievement.[7]

The Expectations of Pupils

Teachers are often conceived as models for the young, sources of values, attitudes, styles of behaviour, as well as intellectual stimulus and enlightenment. The studies we have of this modelling process do not testify to its effectiveness. Inquiries into the nature and source of the socio-moral values of sixteen-year-old boys and girls in 'Prairie City' revealed parents rather than teachers as the moulders of the character of the young. Indeed, teachers appeared to have a negligible influence. The report on this study concludes:

> Another clear implication is that parents cannot reasonably expect to turn over very much of the character training of their children to other people, whether in school, church, or youth organizations. By the very nature of character formation, no one other than parents can ordinarily have one-tenth of their influence; and if the parents are continually re-inforcing their own influence by their day-to-day treatment of the child, other adults can have little expectation of outweighing the parents' influence. Dramatic exceptions to this rule are known, to be sure; but they are dramatic precisely because they are so rare and so hard to achieve. No such exceptions occurred in the Prairie City group, during the study.[8]

When the teacher is taken as a model of social attitudes and behaviour, this may be because he is failing to communicate knowledge and promote understanding. Modelling may, in fact, be a retreat from skill acquisition to style acquisition. The more peripheral and irrelevant qualities of the teacher may be seized upon precisely because the intellectual content of his work is difficult to grasp.[9]

The process of modelling is often discussed in terms of 'identification'. An attempt to discover the extent to which English secondary school children 'identify' with their teachers has led to the same conclusion as the American 'Prairie City' inquiry. Wright investigated the self concepts and the perceptions of parents and teachers among 105 last-year secondary modern school boys and girls. He concluded that 'in their last year at school, secondary modern pupils are a good deal less identified with their teachers than with their parents'. Pupils value their teachers mainly for their intellectual abilities; they are little concerned with their more general, human qualities: 'In so far as the pupils do identify with teachers, it is restricted to those aspects of personality which relate to academic achievement. They admire teachers for their cleverness and knowledge. But they do not seem to value them highly as persons.'[10]

Like the report on Prairie City's adolescents, Wright emphasizes the influence of parents rather than teachers: 'it is of interest to note that the opinion sometimes expressed that adolescents are, in general, rejecting parental influence, receives no confirmation here.' Wright is sceptical about the efficiency of the wider, less specialized role that is today ascribed to teachers. He points out that 'there has been a tendency in recent years to place increasing responsibility on the teacher for such things as mental health, attitudes, values and social awareness of adolescents'. There are no indications that pupils expect these services from their teachers or that when they are rendered they have much effect.

In order to explore further pupils' expectations of teachers in the classroom situation, one of the authors of this book conducted an inquiry with some nine hundred children in junior, secondary modern and grammar schools.[11] The purpose of the investigation was to see whether children of different ages, in different types of school, and in schools differently organized, had different expectations of teachers' behaviour. The views of 131 teachers and of 43 college of education students were also obtained on the relative importance of different aspects of the teacher's task.

THE NATURE OF THE INQUIRY

Eight hundred and sixty-six children in twelve junior schools, 401 in four secondary modern schools, and 112 children in one grammar school were asked to write two short essays on 'A Good Teacher' and 'A Poor Teacher'. Between twenty and thirty minutes were allowed for both essays.

The 1,379 essays were analysed for content by 21 teachers. Each teacher analysed a separate batch of essays. Every independent statement made about 'good' and 'poor' teachers was then assigned to one of four categories considered to be descriptive of mutually exclusive areas of a teacher's classroom behaviour. The four categories were: Teacher (T), Discipline (D), Personal Qualities (P), and Organization (O). The meaning to be attached to these categories was clarified in a general discussion with the

21 teachers after a sample of the essays had been read. In the later stages of the inquiry use was made only of the analysis of essays about a 'good' teacher.

The 5,664 statements about a good teacher which had been collected and sorted were used to construct five scales and a check-list of twenty words and phrases. The first scale (A) consisted of six statements: the two most frequently used by children to describe a good teacher's teaching, the two most frequently used to describe his methods of discipline, and the two most frequently used to describe his personal qualities. These six statements were presented in random order for pupils to rank in order of importance. (The items in the scales were not numbered and no headings were given to the scales.)

Scale A
TEACHING, DISCIPLINE AND PERSONALITY
(*a*) A good teacher is fair and just about punishment and has no favourites.
(*b*) A good teacher explains the work you have to do and helps you with it.
(*c*) A good teacher is patient, understanding, kind and sympathetic.
(*d*) A good teacher is cheerful, friendly, good-tempered, and has a sense of humour.
(*e*) A good teacher is firm and keeps order in the classroom.
(*f*) A good teacher encourages you to work hard at your school work.

The second scale (B) consisted of the six statements which most often occurred in the children's essays to describe a good teacher's manner and method of maintaining discipline.

Scale B
MANNER AND METHOD OF DISCIPLINE
(*a*) A good teacher is firm and keeps order in the classroom.
(*b*) A good teacher is fair and just about punishment.
(*c*) A good teacher praises you for behaving well and working hard.
(*d*) A good teacher has no favourites.
(*e*) A good teacher lets you have some of your own way.
(*f*) A good teacher uses the cane or strap when necessary.

Society and the Teacher's Role

Again the scale was to be used without a heading for pupils to rank the items in order of importance.

The third scale (C) consisted of the six statements most frequently used to describe a good teacher's manner and method of teaching.

Scale C
MANNER AND METHOD OF TEACHING
(a) A good teacher encourages you to work hard at school.
(b) A good teacher explains the work you have to do and helps you with it.
(c) A good teacher knows a great deal about the subject he is teaching.
(d) A good teacher gives interesting lessons.
(e) A good teacher gives you time in the lesson to finish your work.
(f) A good teacher marks your work regularly and fairly.

The fourth scale (D) was constructed in a similar manner from statements about a good teacher's personal qualities.

Scale D
TEACHERS' PERSONAL QUALITIES
(a) A good teacher is cheerful and good-tempered.
(b) A good teacher looks nice and dresses well.
(c) A good teacher is well-mannered and polite.
(d) A good teacher is patient, understanding, kind and sympathetic.
(e) A good teacher has a sense of humour.
(f) A good teacher is friendly with children in and out of school.

The last scale (E) related to a good teacher's organizing abilities.

Scale E
TEACHERS' ORGANIZING ABILITIES
(a) A good teacher makes certain that the classroom is tidy and attractive.
(b) A good teacher has work ready for you as soon as you get into the classroom.
(c) A good teacher makes sure you have the pens, paper and books you need.

(*d*) A good teacher lets children help to give out books, pencils and paper.
(*e*) A good teacher knows where to find the things he wants.
(*f*) A good teacher is able to organize all kinds of activities in the classroom.

The check-list consisted of twenty words and phrases which children had used in their essays to describe a 'good' teacher, e.g. 'young', 'has children of his own', 'is like my mother', 'joins in'.[12] The check-list carried the instruction to tick only the words or phrases which describe a good teacher.

The five scales and the check-list were administered in booklet form to 897 schoolchildren: 500 in the fourth year of the junior school, 230 in the second and 167 in the fourth year of the secondary school. Fourteen junior schools, six secondary schools and two grammar schools took part in the inquiry. The schools were in urban and rural areas, and all came under the same local education authority which organizes its schools in the conventional manner and uses orthodox eleven-plus selection procedures.

Scale A was also completed by 131 teachers and 43 first-year students in a mixed college of education. Seventy-seven of the teachers were men, 54 women; 105 were nongraduates, 26 were graduates. Seventy of the teachers taught in junior schools, 61 in secondary schools.

RESULTS OF THE INQUIRY

The 897 schoolchildren showed the importance they attached to the three aspects of a teacher's behaviour (T, D and P) by ranking the statements on Scale A. In the analysis of results, the rankings were inverted, so that the highest score (6) was given to an item ranked first, and the lowest score (1) to an item ranked sixth. The rankings (thus inverted) for each pair of items representing the three areas of the teacher's behaviour were added together. In this manner the weight attached to each pair of items was obtained. The following table shows the weight attached by the schoolchildren to the three areas of behaviour.

All children gave most weight to the good teacher's teaching, least weight to his personal qualities. The only differences among the children were that junior school children placed more

Table 1
Weight Attached by Children to Three Areas of Teacher Behaviour
(Sum of ranks)

Scale A items	Area		Children 4y. J.	Children 2y. S.	Children 4y. S.
$b + f$	Teaching	(T)	4187	1929	1385
$a + e$	Discipline	(D)	3701	1624	1134
$c + d$	Personality	(P)	2612	1277	988
		N	500	230	167
Percentage		T	39·9	39·9	39·5
Distribution		D	35·2	33·6	32·3
		P	24·9	26·4	28·2
Value of X^2 and Level of P			5·6 N.S.	2·6 N.S. 17·7 ***	

emphasis than secondary school children on the good teacher's discipline; and secondary school children placed more weight than juniors on the good teacher's personal qualities, particularly on his being cheerful, good-tempered, and having a sense of humour. Roughly 40 per cent of the 'weight' was given to 'teaching', a third to 'discipline', and a quarter to 'personality'.

The formal organization of the school appeared to influence children's notions of a good teacher. Children in unstreamed junior schools were significantly more concerned with the good teacher's personal qualities, and those in streamed schools were more concerned with his discipline. It is possible that in the relatively informal situation of the unstreamed class, in which the needs of children differing widely in ability must be met, the personal qualities of the teacher are of especial importance.

There was a striking contrast between the children's view of a good teacher and the teacher's view. Whereas the children emphasized 'teaching', the teachers emphasized 'personality'. The graduate teachers gave greater emphasis to teaching, but the college of education students gave even greater emphasis to 'personality' than the nongraduate teachers. The following table shows the weight given by the different groups of teachers and by the college students to the three areas of teacher behaviour.

Table 2
Weight Attached by Teachers to Three Areas of Teacher Behaviour
(Sum of ranks)

Scale A items	Area	Teachers						Students	
		Jun.	Sec.	Men	Women	N'Grd.	Grad.	Jun.	Sec.
$b+f$	T	457	390	502	345	658	189	127	130
$a+e$	D	442	397	479	360	667	172	93	172
$c+d$	P	571	494	636	429	880	185	179	202
	N	70	61	77	54	105	26	19	24
Percentage	T	31.1	30.3	31.1	30.4	29.8	34.6	31.8	25.8
Distribution	D	30.1	31.1	29.6	31.8	30.3	31.5	23.3	34.1
	P	38.8	38.6	39.3	37.8	39.9	33.9	44.9	40.1
Value of X^2 and level of P		2.0 N.S.		1.5 N.S.		7.6 *		12.9 **	

Men and women teachers did not differ significantly in their emphases, nor did teachers in primary and secondary schools. There were no differences among teachers according to the length of their teaching experience.

The small sample of students from a college of education took up a more exaggerated position than practising teachers. They placed the greatest emphasis on a good teacher's personal qualities. The group training to become junior school teachers placed least weight on 'discipline', those training to become secondary teachers placed least weight on 'teaching'.

In analysing the remaining four scales, the weight attached by the different groups of children to the scale items was obtained by summing their rankings. From these 'weights' a rank order of the items in each of the scales was obtained for the various pupil groups. The extent to which one group of children agreed with another in the value they attached to the items in a scale was calculated by using Spearman's rank correlation coefficient (*rho*).

There was a high level of agreement among all the children in their rankings of the items in Scale B (Manner and Method of Discipline). All children ranked first either item (*a*) 'A good teacher is firm', or item (*b*) 'A good teacher is just and fair about punishment'. They ranked sixth item (*e*) 'A good teacher lets you have some of your own way'.

There were some differences in emphasis among girls at different stages of education. Fourth year secondary school girls differed from younger girls in placing weight on the good teacher's having no favourites (ranked first) rather than on being firm (ranked third). The converse was true for younger girls.

In ranking the items on Scale C (Manner and Method of Teaching) secondary school children were in close agreement, but differed markedly from junior children. The latter ranked first item (*a*), the good teacher encouraging them to work hard, while secondary school children ranked this item third or fourth. Secondary school children placed greatest weight on the teacher explaining work. All children ranked item (*c*), the good teacher knowing his subject, second. They ranked sixth item (*e*), the timing of the lesson.

Fourth year secondary school children differed from all the rest in ranking the statements on Scale D ('Teachers' Personal Qualities). All children agreed in ranking item (*b*), the good teacher's appearance, as least in importance, and in placing item (*f*), the good teacher being friendly, first or second. The main difference was in the emphasis fourth year secondary children placed on the good teacher being cheerful and good tempered. This item was ranked second by fourth year secondary children, but only fourth by younger children. Junior school girls placed particular emphasis on the manners and politeness of the good teacher, placing this item first.

Scale E (Teachers' Organizing Abilities) was analysed for junior school children only. Boys and girls were in close agreement in their rankings ($r_s = 0.99$ $P < 0.01$). They both ranked first the good teacher's making sure they had material to work with, and last his willingness to let pupils give out books, pencils and paper.

The items in the check-list which were ticked by more than 50 per cent of at least one group of children were: 'young', 'married', 'has own children', 'man', 'joins in', 'doesn't use the cane', and 'gives little homework'. Only one item, 'joins in' was checked by 50 per cent or more of the children in all the groups. Items checked by fewer than 15 per cent of the children in each of the groups were: 'old', 'woman', 'is like my father', 'is like my mother', 'fat', and 'doesn't join in'. This suggests that children's stereotype of the good teacher is a young, married man with children who gives little homework and no corporal punishment. They may reject as 'good' teachers women, elderly teachers, and those inclined to behave towards them as their parents might.

This inquiry highlights the discrepancy between children's notions of a good teacher, and teachers' notions of a good teacher. Particularly if they were nongraduates, teachers placed great emphasis on the personal qualities of a good teacher; children at all stages placed emphasis on his teaching skills. The need which pupils want teachers to satisfy is above all the need to be taught and to learn.

The contemporary emphasis on 'good personal relationships' in teaching, and on close and sympathetic contact with children, may actually interfere with the teacher's performance of his task as an instructor. In his classic, *The Sociology of Teaching* (1932), Willard Waller maintained that the effective teacher should maintain a marked social distance from his pupils, that he must be 'relatively meaningless as a person'.

Waller's dictum doubtless requires some modification. Yet there is probably a 'curvilinear' relationship between teachers' friendliness to pupils and their effectiveness. When 'expressive' relationships are emphasized unduly, whether in a school or factory, 'instrumental' relationships may be impaired.[13] Insistence on getting the job done might put at risk the friendliness between subordinates and those in authority. Too little friendliness between teachers and taught may well provoke resistances to learning; too much concern with friendliness may mean that more difficult tasks are never seriously attempted.

Chapter Three
THE EXPECTATIONS OF PARENTS

It is fashionable to talk about the importance of co-operation between parents and teachers. The Plowden Report on Primary Schools is eloquent on the subject. 'Co-operation' appears to mean persuading parents to accept the views of teachers. The Plowden Committee, like the teachers whose views they solicited, had no doubt that parents should not 'run the schools'.[1] While the demands of vocal minorities of (mainly middle-class) parents are known to teachers and education authorities, little is known of the demands of parents in different social situations. This chapter reports an inquiry conducted in 1960 by one of the authors of this book into parents' expectations of teachers in contrasted social areas.[2]

THE NATURE OF THE INQUIRY

A survey of parents' expectations of teachers was carried out in two areas of a Midland city. Parents of the children in the last two years of junior schools were selected for investigation. Children of this age (10 and 11 years) were chosen on the assumption that parental interest and curiosity would be at their height, and views on education most fully developed, in this period immediately preceding secondary selection.

One junior school (A) is situated on a large municipal housing estate; the children in the top two years numbered 310. The school has a 'progressive' headmaster; teaching and school organization are informal and there is no excessive concentration on the 'three Rs'. The other junior school is smaller and there were 104 children in the last two years. It serves an expensive residential area of owner-occupied houses. It is a Church of England school favoured by well-to-do Anglican parents of the district. It is far more formal in its teaching and organization, and places more emphasis on the 'three Rs', than school A.

The Expectations of Parents

The two schools were chosen because of the marked social contrast in the areas they serve.

A random sample of one in four names was taken from the school registers with a view to interviewing the parents of these children. The homes of 26 in school B were approached and interviews were carried out in 22; the homes of 62 children in school A were approached and interviews were carried out in 50.

An important feature of the survey was the separate interviewing of husbands and wives. On the estate (Area A) 42 couples were interviewed, five wives whose husbands were either unavailable or refused interview, and three husbands whose wives were either unavailable or refused interview. Thus one or both parents of 50 children (22 boys and 28 girls) were interviewed – 47 mothers and 45 fathers, a total of 92 parents. In the middle-class district (Area B) 18 couples were interviewed and, in addition, four wives whose husbands were not available. Thus one or both parents of 22 children (14 boys and 8 girls) were interviewed: 18 fathers and 22 mothers, a total of 40 parents. Altogether 132 parents in the two areas were interviewed, representing 72 children (36 boys and 36 girls).

The parents in Area A were predominantly 'working class' in the sense that they were engaged in manual or routine non-manual employment. Forty-seven of the 50 children came from homes where the head of household was in the Registrar General's Occupational Class III (skilled manual and routine non-manual employment), Class IV (semi-skilled manual employment) or Class V (unskilled manual employment). In Area B the parents were predominantly white-collar, professional middle class. Nineteen of the 22 children were from households where the head was in Occupational Class I (higher professional and managerial) or Class II (intermediate, semi-professional employment). The following table gives the percentage distribution of occupational classes in the two groups, in the City (1951 Census Report), and in the country. The overlap between the two groups within the city is small.

Parents in Area A were on average younger than parents in Area B:

The average size of family was larger in Area A than in Area B: 3·2 and 2·5 children respectively.

Table 3
Subjects' Social Status

	I	II	III	IV	V
England and Wales	3·3	15·0	52·7	16·2	12·8
City	2·2	13·5	61·1	12·6	10·6
Area A	nil	6·0	66·0	20·0	8·0
Area B	13·6	72·7	13·6	nil	nil

Table 4
Age of Subjects

	Area A	Area B
Fathers	39 years ($n = 45$)	44·5 years ($n = 18$)
Mothers	37 years ($n = 47$)	39 years ($n = 22$)

The author was assisted in the interviewing by fourteen local teachers who were known to him for their interest in problems of educational sociology and who had, in a number of cases, previous interviewing experience and training in field work. Six families were randomly allocated to each member of the team. Preliminary meetings were held to discuss the content of the interviewing schedule, to clear up any possible ambiguities in the wording and purpose of each item, and to standardize procedure at the interviews and in recording the interviewees' responses. All members of the team were clear that they should record as fully as possible all answers that were given and any additional information or opinion that was volunteered: that although some questions might simply be answered 'yes' or 'no' or 'don't know', any elaboration, qualifying comment or reasons given should also be noted. All interviewers were to emphasize to parents that the interviews were unofficial and that answers were not only entirely confidential but anonymous. (A copy of the schedule used in the interviews will be found at the end of the notes to Chapter Three.)

The interviews provided evidence of parents' expectations on three scores: (*a*) relating to children's behaviour, (*b*) relating to academic and scholastic training, and (*c*) relating to curriculum.

The Expectations of Parents

PARENTS' EXPECTATIONS OF TEACHERS IN THE
SPHERE OF BEHAVIOUR TRAINING

Parents were asked to state whether they expected teachers to guide their child's behaviour as well as teach 'school subjects', and those who answered 'Yes' were asked to give details of the kinds of behaviour they expected teachers to encourage. Interviewers were asked to make a full recording of elaborations and qualifications to answers to the first part of the question (5*a*) so that responses could be classified and placed on a five-point scale ranging from strong emphasis on the home's responsibility at one extreme to strong emphasis on the school's at the other. The following are the five groups into which all answers were sorted:

1. Answers which gave the school an emphatic responsibility for children's behaviour, e.g. 'Certainly the school should teach children how to behave – that's what school's for'; 'Definitely yes – it's the teachers' job to teach manners, etc.'

2. Answers which emphasized the school's importance but also mentioned the need for parental assistance, e.g. 'The school is responsible for behaviour to a great extent, but not entirely' and 'The school has a big responsibility, as well as parents'.

3. Answers which stressed the equal partnership between home and school, e.g. 'Fifty-fifty partnership'; 'Home and school should share responsibility equally'; 'Home and school complementary' and 'School's job in school hours, parent's job otherwise'.

4. Answers which emphasized the home's responsibility but also mentioned the need for some support from the school, e.g. 'It's mainly the parents' responsibility but the school should help' and, 'To some extent – but this is mainly the responsibility of the home and parents'.

5. Answers which placed the responsibility for behaviour emphatically on the parents (requiring of the school no more than that it should not undermine parental influence), e.g. 'It is definitely the parents' job to guide behaviour'; 'Definitely no: the school can't do everything and should stick to its job, which is teaching "subjects" '; and 'Teachers should teach – behaviour is the parents' responsibility'.

The two areas were sharply distinguished in their answers: in Area A, 27·7 per cent gave answers which fell into categories 3, 4 or 5, whereas 57·5 per cent in Area B did so.

Table 5
Emphasis on Responsibility of School or Home

	Category 1 (Emphatically School)	2	3 (50-50 Partners)	4	5 (Emphatically Home)
	% (n)	% (n)	% (n)	% (n)	% (n)
Area A (n 9=2)	68·5 (63)	9·8 (9)	1·1 (1)	4·3 (4)	16·3 (15)
Area B (n 4=0)	35·0 (14)	7·5 (3)	17·5 (7)	15·0 (6)	25·0 (10)

There was no tendency in either area for parents who stressed the home's responsibility for behaviour-training to have fewer children than the average: in Area A, 20 parents stressed the home's responsibility as against the school's and their average number of children was 3·1, while the average for the area was 3·2; in Area B, 23 parents stressed the home and their average number of children was 2·5, the same as for all the families in the area.

There was no tendency for working wives in either area to stress the school's responsibility more than non-working wives. In Area A, 75 per cent of the mothers were in full-time or part-time work, in Area B, 14 per cent were at work. Twenty-five per cent of the mothers in Area A who were not at work stressed the home's responsibility (categories 3, 4 or 5) but so did 22·8 per cent of mothers who went out to work. In Area B, all three working mothers stressed the responsibility of the home as against the school, and 58 per cent (11 out of 19) of the non-working mothers.

It is perhaps of interest in this connection, particularly in view of allegations commonly made by teachers, that two other recent inquiries have failed to establish expected harmful influences of mothers' going out to work. Elizabeth Frazer could find in her inquiry in Aberdeen into the influence of social background on children's attainment at the secondary school 'no evidence to show that children of working mothers are handicapped in their secondary school work'. There were indications that 'if there is any difference at all, it appears to be very slightly in favour of the children whose mothers go out to work, especially in the

The Expectations of Parents

middle ranges of intelligence'.[3] Inquiries among over 5,000 pre-school children have failed to establish that the young child with mother at work suffers from greater emotional instability than others: 'So far, then, there is no reason to believe that the children of employed mothers are in any way at a disadvantage.'[4]

The difference in expectations of teachers between the two areas of the present inquiry reflects their different social class composition. When the same social levels in the two areas are compared the differences disappear. In order to obtain social groups large enough for comparison, Occupational Classes I and II are combined to form the 'Middle Class' and Occupational Classes III, IV and V to form the 'Working Class'. In Area A, three out of five middle-class parents placed emphasis on the home, in Area B, 22 out of 34. There was no significant difference between the two areas within the middle class.[5] On the estate, 17 working-class parents emphasized the home and 70 emphasized the school; in the contrasted area one working-class parent emphasized the home and five the school. There was no significant difference between the two areas within the working class.[6] On the other hand, there was a highly significant difference between the two areas when social class was not held constant. On the estate, 20 parents emphasized the home and 72 the school, in Area B, 23 emphasized the home and 17 the school.[7]

Although in working-class Area A a far higher proportion of parents than in middle-class Area B emphasized the teachers' responsibility for behaviour-training, a far higher proportion claimed explicitly to direct or influence their children's behaviour in three main directions: towards their teachers, towards their friends, and in their choice of friends and associates:

Table 6
Parents' Claims to Direct Behaviour

	Area A (No.) %	Area B (No.) %
Claiming to advise helpful and co-operative attitude to teachers	(79) 85·8	(20) 50
Claiming to advise on behaviour towards other children	(76) 86·2	(26) 65
Claiming to advise on choice of friends	(33) 36·0	(7) 18

Claims to give explicit direction and guidance on behaviour were significantly greater in the working-class than in the middle-class area: in the former 188 claims (out of a possible 276) were made on three criteria; in the latter only 53 (out of a possible 120). The difference is significant at the 0·001 level.[8]

The reasons for this marked difference between the areas was apparent in the answers given by the respondents: parents in the middle-class area were sufficiently confident of their children's behaviour that they felt no need to instruct them on their relationship with teachers and friends, and they felt sufficient confidence in the social composition of the school and the locality that they saw no need to guide their children in the choice of friends. This was clear from many of the answers given to questions 7a and 7c. The interviewees were not asked *why* they did or did not advise their children about whom to play with or whom to avoid: the questions could be answered simply 'Yes' or 'No', yet one-third of the parents who said that they did not tell their children how to behave with other children volunteered the explanation that this was 'unnecessary' and a similar proportion of those who said they never told their children not to play with certain other children elaborated their answer by saying that there was no need to do so in this school and/or district: 'No: the children at this school are nice children' and 'No: it is unnecessary around here'. The marked difference, then, between directing and non-directing parents is a function of area and not of social class. The greater tendency among parents of working-class Area A to direct behaviour reflects their lack of confidence in the social contacts available to their children.

BEHAVIOUR WHICH TEACHERS SHOULD ENCOURAGE

The greater emphasis in working-class Area A on the school's responsibility for behaviour-training does not necessarily reflect a lack of concern for parental duties: the school is often given the job of directing behaviour because, it is felt, only the school can do this effectively. The reason often volunteered for assigning so much responsibility to the school was that the children would 'take more notice of teachers' than of parents.

The anxiety over children's disobedience towards parents is reflected in answers to the question: 'What kinds of behaviour

The Expectations of Parents

do you expect the school to encourage in your child?' Parents who expected teachers to guide behaviour were asked to particularize. Out of the 77 parents in Area A who gave such particulars of the attitudes, virtues, and qualities of personality which they wished the school to develop, 70 per cent showed a concern for various forms of unruly or anti-social behaviour. Fifty-two per cent specified training in obedience, respect for elders, or 'not to be cheeky', and a further 18 per cent stated honesty, 'steadiness', truthfulness, respectability, or 'curbing of bad language'. (A further 20 per cent expected the school to teach 'manners' which also appears to mean very largely, if not exclusively, respect for elders and acceptance of adult authority.) Training in cleanliness was mentioned by five of the 77 parents. More 'secondary' virtues were less frequently mentioned as requiring attention and encouragement by teachers: 'lady-like behaviour' was mentioned once, as were 'tolerance', 'the standards of society', and 'eloquent speech'.

In middle-class Area B there was not so much stress on training in obedience and respect for elders, probably because such training was unnecessary. Thirty parents detailed types of behaviour which they wished teachers to foster. The following were mentioned in Area B but not by parents in Area A: fair play (4), punctuality (3), self-confidence (2), sociability (1), diligence (1), tidiness (1), etiquette (1), 'virtues of a good citizen' (1), and 'character' (1). The following which had been mentioned in Area A were also mentioned in Area B: good manners (7), obedience and/or 'respect' (4), politeness (1), cleanliness (1), tolerance (1), and 'gentlemanly behaviour' (1).

PARENTS' ADVICE ON HOW TO BEHAVE WITH OTHER CHILDREN AND ON WHOM TO AVOID AS PLAYMATES

Seventy-six parents (82 per cent) in Area A claimed that they advised their children on how they should behave towards their friends, and 26 parents (65 per cent) in the middle-class district. Parents in both areas told their sons not to fight and not to bully, to show self-restraint and not to be provoked into quarrelling. In Area B, however, parents were concerned that their children should be more sociable, in Area A that they should be less. Middle-class parents were urging their 10-year-old boys and girls to 'Try to fit in' and to 'Mix with the crowd'. One father had visited his son's headmaster to discuss how they might 'draw him out of his reticence'. No working-class parent had any such concern: on the contrary, they were anxious that their boys should 'keep out of gangs' and that their girls should 'keep away from strangers' and not 'stray away'. Working-class parents urged some of the less gregarious virtues ('Don't ape others' and 'Make your own decisions'), but no middle-class parent did so. Such advice clearly reflected the disquiet of working-class parents at the gregariousness of their children and their association in play-groups beyond effective parental control.

Few middle-class parents (18 per cent) felt the need to advise their children about playmates to avoid: those who gave advice mostly did so in general terms ('Don't play with ill-mannered and badly behaved children'); one father advised his daughter not to play with children who spoke badly, three fathers advised their sons to avoid 'toughs' and bullies.

Thirty-six per cent of the parents on the housing estate (17 mothers and 16 fathers) warned their children specifically against children who steal (or who are on probation or in trouble with the police) (7), who are cheeky (5), bullies (3), older than themselves (3), dirty (2), destructive (2), or 'grammar-school snobs' (1). Ten gave more general advice to keep clear of trouble-makers.

PARENTS' EXPECTATIONS REGARDING SCHOLASTIC TRAINING

There was a social class difference in the preference expressed for a grammar school education similar in magnitude to that found in earlier inquiries in this field.[9] Fifty-four point three per cent of the parents in working-class Area A preferred the grammar school for their children, 90 per cent in Area B. The details are given in the following table:

In the middle-class area mothers and fathers were equally ambitious for their children, and for their daughters as much as their sons: they preferred a grammar-school education for their children regardless of sex. It has been suggested in some inquiries that in working-class areas this is not the case, that parents, and particularly fathers, are more ambitious for their sons than for their daughters.[10] The present inquiry does not support this view.

The Expectations of Parents

Table 7
Parents' Secondary School Preferences

Preferred School	Area A (No.)	%	Area B (No.)	%
Grammar	(50)	54·3	(36)	90·0
Modern	(16)	17·4	(2)	5·0
Technical	nil	nil	(1)	2·5
E.S.N.	nil	nil	(1)	2·5
Comprehensive	(1)	1·1	nil	nil
No preference/don't know	(25)	27·2	nil	nil

There was no significant tendency for either boys or girls to be especially favoured by their parents: 50 grammar school preferences were expressed by parents, 18 directed to 22 boys, and 32 to 28 girls. This difference is not statistically significant.[11] There was no difference in the ambitions of mothers and fathers: 29 out of 47 mothers stated a preference for the grammar school, 21 out of 45 fathers.[12] Fathers did not favour boys: their grammar school preferences were directed to 12 out of 28 girls and to 9 out of 22 boys. There appeared to be a trend for working-class mothers to be more ambitious for their daughters than for their sons: 9 of their grammar school choices went to boys, 20 to girls, 10 of their non-grammar-school choices to boys and 8 to girls. This difference, however, falls short of statistical significance.[13]

There was a similar degree of realism in both areas in stating a preference for the grammar school. Every parent was asked whether they considered their child to be doing well, fair or badly in his or her school work; those who said 'Well' and had previously stated a preference for the grammar school were considered to be realistic. On this criterion 18·4 per cent were unrealistic in Area A and 12·5 per cent in middle-class Area B.

There was a marked difference between the two areas in the realism of their preferences for the secondary modern school. Lack of realism in this connection was regarded as a choice for the modern school whilst rating the child's school work very good. Twenty-four per cent in Area A were unrealistic in this sense in their choice of the modern school, but only 5 per cent in Area B.

Parents in the two areas differed sharply in their stated reasons for choosing the grammar school. In working-class Area A far greater stress was given to 'prospects' and 'getting on in life', in Area B to 'an education appropriate to the child's interests and abilities'. Reasons given in both areas for choosing the grammar school can be placed in four categories: I, Future Prospects; II, Suited to Abilities/Interests/Aptitudes; III, Better Education; IV, Social Reasons. In Area A 48 reasons were given for preferring the grammar school, 40 in Area B. They are classified as follows:

Table 8
Reasons for Preferring the Grammar School

		Area A	Area B
I Future Prospects	(No.) % e.g.	(26) 54·1 'Better jobs' 'Better chances in life'	(11) 27·5 'Better prospects' 'Needed for professional career'
II Suited to Abilities	(No.) % e.g.	(6) 12·5 'Child clever enough'	(15) 37·5 'Child capable of it' 'Child that way inclined' 'Would suit the child'
III Better Education	(No.) % e.g.	(12) 25 'Better teaching' 'Moulds character' 'Gives confidence' 'Specialist training' 'Better discipline' 'Gives self-assurance' 'More interesting studies'	(9) 22·5 'Better qualified teachers' 'Better discipline' 'Wider curriculum'
IV Social Reasons	(No.) % e.g.	(4) 8·4 'High social tone of companions' 'Get away from Estate' 'Better social standing' 'Better children there'	(5) 12·5 'Higher social standing' 'Family has always been to grammar schools' 'Child's friends and relations at grammar schools'

The working-class area was far more 'permissive' in its attitude than the middle-class area: 27 per cent of the parents expressed no preference for a particular type of secondary education, merely saying: 'Wherever the child will be happy', 'Whatever he/she wants', or even: 'The child to choose'. Twice as many fathers (16) showed such permissiveness (or indifference).

It is of some interest in this connection that the permissiveness of parents in Area A as compared with Area B was also apparent from their attitude to school discipline. All parents were asked: 'Do you think the teachers should "stand over" the children more and "keep them at it"?' Although in Area B the school is run on formal lines with intensive preparation for examinations, 55 per cent of the parents answered 'Yes'; in Area A, where the school is much more informal, only 37 per cent said 'Yes'. In Area B 27·5 per cent said 'No', in Area A 63 per cent (17·5 per cent of the answers in Area B were too qualified and equivocal for classification).

A striking difference between the attitudes and expectations of mothers and fathers was a feature of working-class Area A but not of Area B. In Area B all the married couples agreed in their secondary school preferences, although husbands and wives were interviewed separately; in Area A 28·6 per cent of the couples were in disagreement: 3 fathers chose the grammar school when their wives chose the modern school or had no preference; but 9 mothers chose the grammar school for their children when their husbands chose the modern school or expressed no preference.

There was a strong indication of the greater general interest and concern of working-class mothers, as compared with fathers, in the frequency of their visits to the school.[14] When all parents of both areas were compared, there was a highly significant difference between Area A and Area B: 47·7 per cent in Area A claimed to have attended the last Parents' Evening, 85 per cent in Area B.[15] But in the middle-class area there was no significant difference between husbands and wives (16 fathers attended, 18 mothers); in the other area there was a marked difference: 13 fathers attended and 31 mothers.[16]

Not only did parents in Area A visit the school less frequently than parents in Area B, but they knew the name of the headmaster and of the class teacher less often.[17] In Area A 26·1 per cent of parents did not know the headmaster's name, and 35·8 per cent did not know the class teacher's name; in Area B no parent was ignorant of the headmaster's name and two (5 per cent) did not know the class teacher's. The difference between the two areas is highly significant.[18]

PARENTS' EXPECTATIONS OF THE CURRICULUM

Parents were asked whether they thought 'too little attention is being given to reading, writing and arithmetic in the education of your child' and also whether they thought other subjects, apart from the '3 Rs', were being neglected. There was no difference between the two areas in the amount of satisfaction-dissatisfaction expressed in their answers to these questions. In Area A 45·6 per cent of the parents considered that the 3 Rs and/or other subjects were neglected, in Area B 57·5 per cent.[19]

A greater dissatisfaction with the teaching of the 3 Rs was expressed in the middle-class district (50 per cent of the parents), yet the school attended by their children is comparatively formal, placing great emphasis on the 3 Rs. In the second area, where the school is less formal and less pre-occupied with the 3 Rs, only 31·5 per cent of the parents thought that too little attention was being given to reading, writing and arithmetic.

In the middle-class district 27·5 per cent thought that other subjects were either neglected or important but omitted from the curriculum. Five subjects were mentioned, in all 20 times: they were all verbal-academic-literary in character. Geography was mentioned 8 times, history 6, 'nature' twice, 'general knowledge' twice, and a foreign language twice.

In the working-class estate 18 parents (19·4 per cent) thought other subjects were neglected. The great majority of subjects or activities mentioned were non-verbal, practical, physical. Swimming was mentioned 5 times, arts and crafts twice, First Aid once, cookery for boys once, physical education once, and sewing once. Verbal-academic skills were mentioned only three times: elocution, science and history. Eight parents also mentioned religion, whilst none did so in Area B. Whereas the mention of other subjects is probably a reflection of the interests of the parents rather than the condition of the schools,[20] the fact that in Area B no mention was made of religion is perhaps a reflection of the strong religious emphasis which this Church of England school is known to have.

In the middle-class area 41 per cent of the children learned skills outside school hours for which their parents paid, whilst only 18 per cent of the children in Area A received such paid tuition. In Area A 5 children learned dancing, 3 music and 1

The Expectations of Parents

horse-riding; in Area B 4 children learned swimming, 3 music, 2 dancing, 1 horse-riding and 1 elocution.

AREA AND CLASS DIFFERENCES IN EXPECTATIONS

In summary, then, parents in the two areas were sharply distinguished in their expectations of teachers in the junior school. On the municipal housing estate parents tended to place more responsibility on the school for training the child's behaviour – in part, at least, because they felt that teachers were more effective than themselves; in the well-to-do residential area parents placed more emphasis on the home. Working mothers and mothers with large families did not place more emphasis on the school than non-working mothers and mothers with small families.

The difference in attitude towards the responsibilities of parents and teachers in the two areas reflects their social class composition. But other differences between the two groups of parents must be interpreted as a function of locality rather than of social class, in particular the greater tendency on the estate for parents to give directions (however ineffectual) to their children regarding the choice of playmates and their behaviour towards their teachers and friends. Parents in the well-to-do area felt sufficient confidence in the social composition of the school and of the locality to make such directions superfluous.

Parents in Area A wanted teachers to encourage more 'basic' behaviour such as cleanliness and obedience – and behaviour which would support adult authority; parents in Area B mentioned more 'secondary' virtues such as diligence, and punctuality. Middle-class parents wanted their children to 'mix', working-class parents wanted theirs to be less gregarious.

Parents on the estate were less ambitious for their children in terms of preferred type of secondary schooling, and those who expressed a preference for the grammar school tended to do so for different reasons from those advanced by middle-class parents: the former stressed 'prospects', the latter the appropriateness of the education to the interests and abilities of the child. Parents in both areas were equally realistic in choosing the grammar school, but working-class parents were often unrealistic in their choice of the modern school for their children.

In the working-class area parents visited the school and knew the headmaster's and the class teacher's names far less often than in the contrasted area; and in the working-class area fathers had visited the school less often than mothers. There was, however, no conclusive evidence that working-class mothers were more ambitious for their children's secondary education than their husbands. Married couples were in agreement about their children's secondary education less often than in the middle-class district.

Both groups of parents were equally satisfied or dissatisfied with the content and emphasis of the school curriculum, but whereas middle-class parents considered that academic-verbal-literary subjects were neglected, parents on the estate tended to allege that practical-physical-applied subjects and activities were neglected. This was probably a more accurate reflection of parental interests, values and pre-occupations than of conditions in the schools concerned.

Chapter Four
TEACHERS' ROLE CONFLICTS

The teacher's job is ill-defined and open to a variety of interpretations, in consequence teachers experience 'role conflict'. They perceive different demands and expectations from various groups of people who are important to them – parents, pupils, their own colleagues and headteachers. This chapter reports the authors' study[1] of the conflicts which teachers experience in the performance of their work.

In large-scale and quickly changing societies conflicts are common in all walks of life. General medical practitioners appear to be suffering from considerable uncertainty about their proper role and often to experience demands which they cannot regard as legitimate. Teachers may be less affected than the members of many professions particularly in newly developed fields of social work. But changes in the organization of education and more general processes of social change are combining to make a troubled teaching profession.

Contemporary changes in the status and function of teachers arise from the deliberate policy decisions of Government and other educational authorities. It would be premature to assess the consequences for teachers of school reorganization according to some variant of the comprehensive principle. But there can be little doubt that where such reorganization has occurred or is planned, grammar-school teachers in particular feel that their status is threatened, and are uncertain and anxious about their new role. In extreme cases role uncertainty and conflict may lead to flight from the profession or from schools into sectors of education – like the colleges of education – which appear to maintain one's former status and afford familiar and unambiguous roles.

Quite apart from the problems raised by reorganization, there are clear signs that more general processes of social change are raising acute problems for some teachers. Thus changes in family life impinge on the work of teachers in many ways. Mothers increasingly go to work and 'maternal' functions may be expected of teachers. Some working mothers are themselves teachers and may feel conflict between their family and professional obligations.

Wilson has argued that many social changes today pose especially acute problems for teachers (as opposed, say, to surgeons or barristers).[2] He claims that teachers must put more of themselves into their work at a time when other professional roles are becoming 'affectively neutral'; that the demands made upon them become more diverse as they take over more of the duties of parents; and yet the requirements of the job, and particularly the criteria of success, are often ambiguous, conflicting, lacking in definition. Different people affected by and concerned with the teacher's work may make different and conflicting demands upon him.

This last point has been made by Mays – not from general impression, but from actual investigation of back-street schools in Liverpool. Thus one of Her Majesty's Inspectors may criticize teachers for neglecting social training, but a local authority inspector may urge more concern with examination results. 'As a result of such confusion of advice and lack of any authoritative policy, the final decision must be left to the school itself, and the main burden will inevitably fall on the shoulders of the headteacher. But even he cannot do much either way without the co-operation and agreement of his colleagues which may not be easy to obtain.'[3]

A teacher forms a notion of his job, the objectives he should pursue and the priorities he should attach to them, from his professional training and experience in the school. He learns what is expected of him – and 'human conduct is in part a function of expectations'.[4] 'A person cannot enact a role for which he lacks the necessary role expectations. These must be acquired through experience.'[5] But the conduct and priorities the teacher has learned in training may not accord with the demands and expectations of his colleagues, headmaster and pupils when he joins the school. In particular he may have learned to attach more importance to 'good personal relationships', and less to instruction and imparting a body of knowledge, than headmasters or even colleagues and pupils attach to them.

Schools, like other social organizations, confront their members with adaptive dilemmas and these can be examined in terms of 'role-set'[6] and of 'role-demands', 'role-conception' and 'role-performance'.[7] A person occupying a particular status (as teacher, wife, foreman, son, etc.) may perceive demands and expectations that he should behave in ways which are at odds with his own conception of his role; and neither his ideal image nor the expectations of others may match his actual role performance. The size of the discrepancy between these role-demands, role-conception and role-performance is a measure of the conflict experienced by a person occupying a particular status. The picture may be still more complicated, for the role-demands made by different individuals and groups are not necessarily in agreement: the 'role-set' usually implies an array of conflicting expectations.

There is a distinction between role-role (or inter-role) conflict and conflict which occurs in the enactment of a single role (intra-role conflict). Sarbin speaks of role conflict in the former sense, as discrepancy between two or more roles which a person may attempt to fulfil: 'Role conflict occurs when a person occupies two or more positions simultaneously and when the role expectations of one are incompatible with the role expectations of the other.'[8] There are indications in the work of Gross that intra-role conflicts have more bearing on a person's performance of his job. In his study of the role conflicts of the American school superintendent, Gross found that job-satisfaction was unrelated to inter-role conflict. (Thus problems of hiring and promoting teachers were related to job satisfaction, but problems of demands on his time – which affected his role as husband and father – were not.)[9] Consequently, in the inquiry reported in this chapter, an attempt was made to estimate teachers' intra-role, but not their inter-role, conflicts.

No more is attempted here than a mapping of the areas of conflict, and the authors are aware of the need for follow-up studies which relate levels of role-conflict to teachers' efficiency and morale. But there are indications in empirical research carried out in America that high levels of conflict reduce efficiency. Thus a study of officer-instructors at a military academy showed how the intensity of conflict was associated with teaching effectiveness (as measured by the ratings of colleagues).[10] Of course people learn to live with their conflicts, and often to minimize them by denying the legitimacy of some of the demands which are made upon them; but people who perceive diverse demands from legitimate sources are likely to be disturbed and unhappy and less assured in the performance of their work.

The intention of the present inquiry was not only to measure levels of conflict among different categories of teacher, but to establish its principal sources and its variations according to type of school, the social-class composition of the school's area, and the age, sex, experience and qualifications of teachers. Thus it was expected that in secondary modern schools, with their relatively brief history and still uncertain objectives and status, conflict might be more widespread than in grammar schools. It was also expected that teachers in working-class districts might experience more conflict than their colleagues working in middle-class areas.

Teachers who obtain a university degree have commonly aspired to grammar school teaching; but many are now employed in secondary modern schools. It was expected that their role-conflicts might be great, since they are engaged in relatively low-level academic work when their qualifications are relatively high. It was also expected that married women teachers might show more signs of conflict (particularly *vis-à-vis* headteachers) than unmarried; and teachers of non-academic subjects in grammar schools more than teachers of subjects carrying high prestige such as languages and mathematics.

Teachers were expected to feel at odds with their pupils, and perhaps with parents and colleagues, over the importance, or lack of importance, they attached to 'discipline'; and in secondary modern schools conflict with pupils was expected over the importance attached to 'teaching' in the sense of serious and efficient instruction. The markedly hierarchical and even authoritarian character of schools particularly at the secondary stage suggested that assistant teachers might often feel that their views conflicted with the headteacher's over many areas of a teacher's professional activities.

THE NATURE OF THE INQUIRY

In the attempt to measure teachers' conflicts a technique was employed which one of the authors had previously devised to assess the conflicts of adolescents.[11] A questionnaire was constructed based on the description of the teacher's function which was used above in Chapter two. The four main aspects of the teacher's role – 'discipline', 'teaching', 'personality', and 'organization' –

were listed with illustrative phrases (see Fig. 1). They were to be ranked by samples of teachers as they ideally valued them ('role conception'), as they thought the head of the school, their colleagues, parents and their pupils respectively valued them in their performance ('role expectations'), and finally as they thought these four areas of teacher-behaviour in fact characterized their work ('perceived role performance'). By comparing the extent of agreement among the ranks (using Kendall's coefficient of concordance),[12] a measure of role conflict for each teacher could be obtained.

	D1	T2	P3	O4
(Role conception)	Ideal self			
	Head Teacher			
(Role set)	Colleagues			
	Parents			
	Pupils			
(Perceived role performance)	Actual self			

1 *Discipline:* e.g. 'firm and keeps children quiet and orderly'/'has no favourites' etc.
2 *Teaching:* e.g. 'explains work clearly'/'gives interesting lessons', etc.
3 *Personality:* e.g. 'patient, understanding, kind, sympathetic', etc.
4 *Organization:* e.g. 'has everything ready for the lesson'/'always knows where to find things he/she wants', etc.

Fig. 1. Teacher attributes ranked by subjects for self and others

(Although this questionnaire is based on the work reported in Chapter two, it differs from the questionnaires described there in structure and presentation. It was used for a different purpose – to provide a standard instrument for assessing role-conflict which could be used across schools of different types. Direct comparisons cannot therefore be made between the findings on teachers' role conceptions reported here and in Chapter two.)

The assumption made in the present inquiry is that the conflict of ranks is a fair indication of conflict actually felt. This is no more than an assumption, but seems reasonable in the light of work done by numerous investigators using rating devices such as Osgood's semantic differential.[13] Conflict between self- and super-ego, for example, has been measured by comparing the rankings of various attributes as valued by subjects and as subjects perceive their fathers to value them. 'Semantic distances' have been calculated as an indication of conflict between self and friends, or as a measure of guilt feelings. The present research similarly assumes that discrepant rankings are valid measures of conflicts.

Three local education authorities were randomly selected and approached for permission to conduct the inquiry in their schools. Four grammar schools co-operated (two mixed, one boys' and one girls') and 14 secondary modern schools (nine mixed, three boys' and two girls'). Two hundred and sixty-three teachers completed the questionnaire, 185 in secondary modern schools (101 men and 84 women), and 78 in grammar schools (41 men and 37 women). The average age of the male grammar school teachers was 40 years, of the female teachers 37 years; of the male teachers in secondary modern schools 39 years, and of the female teachers 34 years.

At the primary level 17 junior schools co-operated (137 teachers: 47 men and 90 women) and 10 infant schools (48 teachers, all women).

One purpose of the inquiry was to establish differences in teachers' role-conflicts according to the social-class composition of the area in which they worked. Primary schools only were used in this connection and this chapter reports on primary school teachers' role-conflicts only with reference to the social context. Grammar and modern schools served scattered catchment areas and social classification of the districts in which they were located was either impossible or unrealistic.

In consequence the secondary school teachers' completed questionnaires are fully analysed below but the results are not related to any social-class considerations. All teachers at the secondary stage who completed the questionnaire did not complete all six ratings. The 263 teachers had between them 1,578 columns to complete. In fact they completed 1,527 (96·9 per cent). The teachers were in some cases unable or unwilling to rate the expectations of their colleagues on the grounds that they were too various to permit generalization. Others refrained from rating the expectations of parents on the grounds that they had too little contact with them and knowledge of their views. Nevertheless, the overwhelming majority did feel able to make these ratings. Half of the columns which were not completed relate to self: 23 teachers were unable or unwilling to evaluate their own teaching performance, although they had no difficulty, apparently, in evaluating the expectations of head, colleagues, pupils and parents.

CONFLICTS IN THE SECONDARY SCHOOLS

When a teacher's rankings were in very close agreement (indicated by a coefficient of concordance above the 1 per cent level of significance) he was judged to experience little role-conflict; when his rankings were somewhat less in accord (indicated by a coefficient between the 1 per cent and 5 per cent levels of significance) he was judged to experience medium conflicts; when the rankings showed little agreement (indicated by a coefficient below the 5 per cent level), he was judged to be in high conflict. A third of the secondary modern school teachers suffered from high conflict measured and defined in this way, but only 26·9 per cent of the grammar school teachers. Seventeen point eight per cent of the former were in low conflict, 32·1 per cent of the latter.[14]

There were no significant differences between grammar school men and women, but modern school men were found less often at the extremes of conflict than their female colleagues: a small proportion had a high level of measured conflict, but a small proportion, too, had a low level of measured conflict. Twenty-five point seven per cent compared with 42·8 per cent were in high conflict, 14·9 per cent compared with 21·5 per cent in low conflict.

The degree of conflict did not vary with age. Men teachers under the age of 36 were compared with those over, 53·6 per cent of the former were found to have coefficients below 0·5, 56 per cent of the latter.

There were no differences between teachers in single-sex and mixed schools. Graduates in secondary modern schools were not more often in conflict than their non-graduate colleagues.

When different subject specialists were compared, mathematicians in both secondary modern and grammar schools were found to be significantly over-represented among high scores (low conflict). There were 27 mathematics specialists: 19 had coefficients over 0·5, 8 below.[15] Teachers of domestic science, on the other hand, were significantly over-represented among low scores (high conflict). There were 16 teachers of domestic science; only 2 had coefficients over 0·5.[16] Conflict appeared to centre principally around the evaluation of 'personality' in the teacher's role. When the rankings of the 14 teachers whose scores indicated high conflict were summed for each area of behaviour, the following results were obtained for 'personality':

Table 9
Domestic Science Teachers' Evaluation of Personality

	Ideal Self	Head	Colleagues	Parents	Pupils	Actual Self
Sum of Ranks	39	54	43	35	23	33

(A theoretical minimum of 14 could be obtained if all the teachers agreed in rating personality first for one of the sources, a theoretical maximum of 56 if all agreed on rating it fourth for a particular source.)

Clearly, the teachers of domestic science gave only intermediate weight to 'personality' (they gave the greatest weight to 'teaching'), but they saw their pupils as attaching great weight to it, and the headteacher very little. Conversely, in the case of 'discipline', to which they also attached intermediate importance, they saw the head as giving very great weight and their pupils very little. The particular areas of conflict (D and P) are the same as for other teachers, but their conflicts are more extreme.

SOURCES OF CONFLICT

Tables 10 to 13 and Figs. 2 and 3 show where the teachers saw the main weight of expectation from pupils, parents, headteachers and colleagues; the aspects of the teacher's job which they themselves rated most important; and the aspects which they thought in fact most characterized their performance. All groups of teachers placed the greatest emphasis on 'teaching' and saw others placing great weight on this function. All placed least weight on 'organization', although all except women teachers in grammar schools saw the headteacher having moderately strong expectations in this direction.

Most conflict was experienced over the part that 'discipline' and 'personality' play in the work of a teacher. In particular teachers in grammar schools rate 'discipline' low but see others rating it high. Marked discrepancies appear in the perceived evaluations of 'personality'. Men teachers in grammar schools saw headteachers attaching very little weight to 'personality', but they themselves valued it highly. (Women teachers in secondary modern schools also judged the headteacher's emphasis on 'personality' to be slight.)

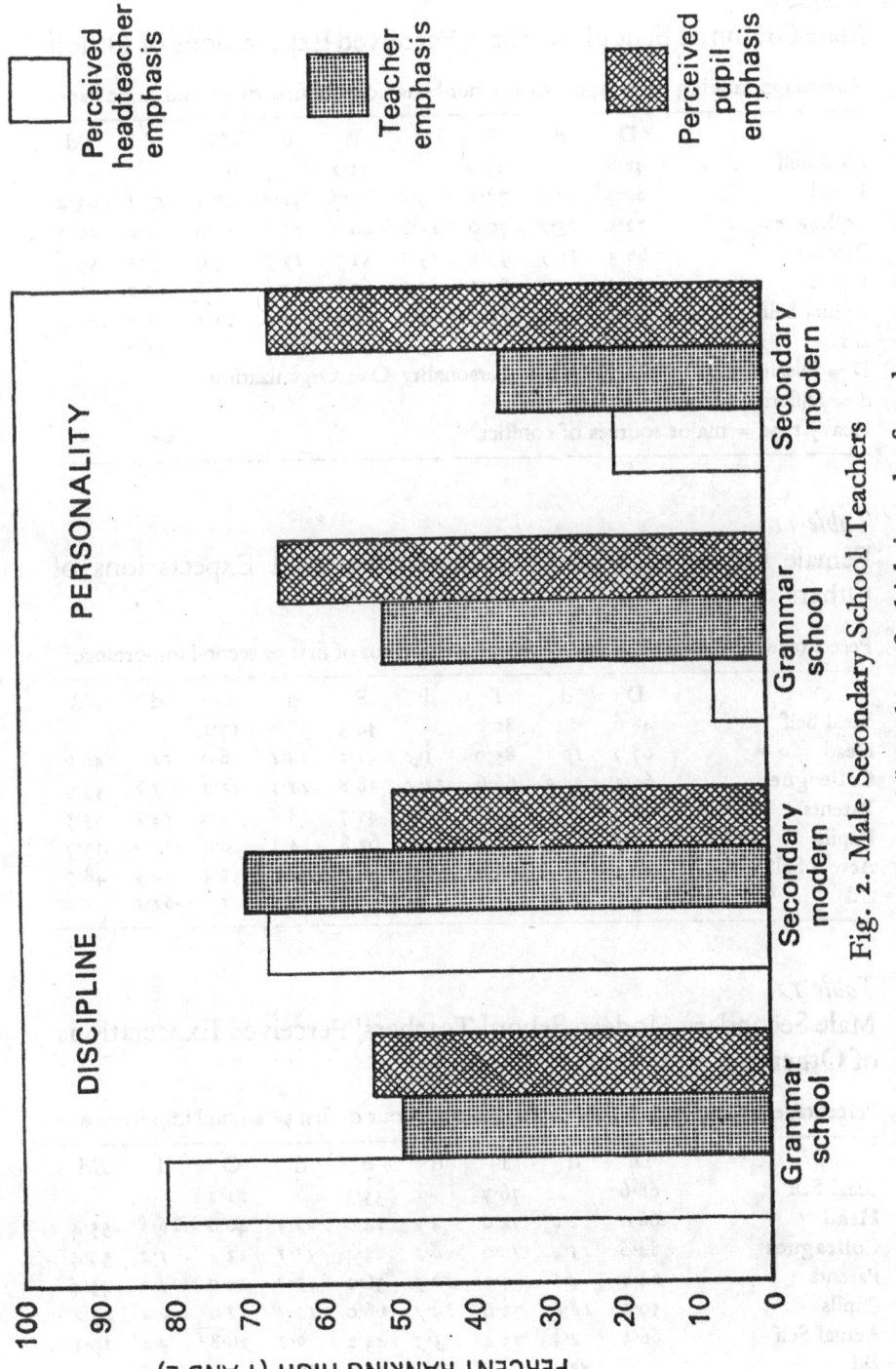

Fig. 2. Male Secondary School Teachers

This is one of two diagrams. The other of which is to be found on page 57.

Table 10
Male Grammar School Teachers' Perceived Expectations of Others

Percentage ranking each aspect of teacher-behaviour of first or second importance

	D	d	T	d	P	d	O	d	Σd
Ideal Self	48·8		83·0		51·2		12·2		
Head	80·5	*31·7*	78·1	*4·9*	9·7	*41·5*	29·3	*17·1*	**95·2**
Colleagues	72·5	*23·7*	70·0	*13·0*	40·0	*11·2*	15·0	*2·8*	50·7
Parents	68·3	*19·5*	97·2	*14·2*	31·7	*19·5*	4·9	*7·3*	59·5
Pupils	52·5	*3·7*	80·0	*3·0*	65·0	*13·8*	2·5	*10·0*	30·5
Actual Self	63·2	*14·4*	64·7	*18·3*	57·9	*6·7*	13·2	*1·0*	40·4
Σd		*93·0*		*53·4*		*92·7*		*28·2*	

D = Discipline T = Teaching P = Personality O = Organization
d = Difference from Ideal Self
Heavy type = major sources of conflict

Table 11
Female Grammar School Teachers' Perceived Expectations of Others

Percentage ranking each aspect of teacher-behaviour of first or second importance

	D	d	T	d	P	d	O	d	Σd
Ideal Self	48·6		80·0		54·3		17·1		
Head	67·7	*19·1*	85·0	*5·3*	41·2	*13·1*	6·0	*11·1*	48·6
Colleagues	69·5	*20·9*	66·6	*13·4*	38·8	*15·5*	22·2	*5·1*	**53·9**
Parents	60·0	*11·4*	91·4	*11·4*	45·7	*8·6*	3·0	*14·1*	45·5
Pupils	51·4	*2·5*	85·7	*5·7*	62·8	*8·5*	0·0	*17·0*	33·7
Actual Self	31·4	*17·2*	88·6	*8·6*	45·7	*8·6*	31·4	*14·3*	48·7
Σd		*71·1*		*44·4*		*53·9*		*61·1*	

Table 12
Male Secondary Modern School Teachers' Perceived Expectations of Others

Percentage ranking each aspect of teacher-behaviour of first or second importance

	D	d	T	d	P	d	O	d	Σd
Ideal Self	68·6		76·7		35·3		21·2		
Head	66·0	*2·6*	72·0	*4·7*	24·0	*29·3*	40·0	*18·8*	**55·4**
Colleagues	84·0	*15·4*	70·0	*6·7*	22·4	*31·1*	22·4	*1·2*	**54·4**
Parents	64·0	*4·6*	89·0	*12·3*	36·0	*17·3*	10·0	*11·2*	45·4
Pupils	50·0	*18·6*	72·0	*4·7*	66·0	*12·7*	12·0	*9·2*	45·2
Actual Self	66·3	*2·3*	73·4	*3·3*	44·2	*9·1*	16·8	*4·4*	19·1
Σd		*43·5*		*31·7*		*99·5*		*44·8*	

Table 13
Female Secondary Modern School Teachers' Perceived Expectations of Others

Percentage ranking each aspect of teacher-behaviour of first or second importance

	D	d	T	d	**P**	d	O	d	Σd
Ideal Self	61·9		84·5		33·3		21·4		
Head	84·5	22·6	67·8	16·7	11·9	21·4	36·9	15·5	76·2
Colleagues	76·2	14·3	64·3	20·2	30·9	2·4	27·4	6·0	43·9
Parents	65·4	3·5	91·7	7·2	39·3	6·0	8·3	13·1	29·8
Pupils	42·8	19·1	72·6	11·9	75·0	42·7	11·9	9·5	63·2
Actual Self	64·0	2·1	82·6	1·9	41·3	18·0	14·7	6·7	28·7
Σd		61·6		57·9		70·5		50·8	

Men teachers in grammar schools differed significantly from women teachers in perceiving the headteacher's lighter emphasis on personality, but they saw the headteachers as attaching more weight to organization. They rated discipline as a marked feature of their teaching more often than the women.

Men teachers in secondary modern schools differed significantly from their female colleagues in their perception of the headteacher's evaluation of 'personality': they saw him (or her) more often as attaching importance to it.[17] And the women teachers in the modern schools did not ascribe to the head the same concern for 'personality' as did their counterparts in grammar schools;[18] and they more frequently rated 'discipline' as an outstanding feature of their own performance as teachers.[19]

Men teachers in grammar schools put less emphasis on 'discipline' in their picture of their ideal selves than did men teachers in modern schools.[20] They were significantly more inclined to see their colleagues placing emphasis on 'personality'.[21]

The discrepancy between teachers' 'ideal selves' and their perceptions of headteachers' expectations occurred principally over 'discipline' and 'personality'. Headteachers' emphasis on 'discipline' was seen (by all except men teaching in secondary modern schools) to be greater than the teachers' ideal emphasis; all groups perceived his emphasis on personality to be less.

Both men and women in both types of school were poised, in their ideal conception of their roles, between the perceived expectations of their pupils regarding 'personality', on the one hand, and the quite contrary perceived emphasis of headteachers on the other. Men teachers in grammar schools in particular placed far more emphasis on 'personality' than they thought the head did, and women teachers in modern schools far less than they thought their pupils did.

CONFLICT AND THE SOCIAL CONTEXT

The conflicts of teachers in primary schools were examined with special reference to the social character of the schools' catchment areas. The *degree* of conflict was significantly related to the social context. (The sources of conflict were similar to those found at the secondary stage – namely, the evaluation of 'personality' and the perceived expectations of headteachers. Both infant and junior teachers saw the headteacher as attaching little weight to 'personality', although infant school teachers thought she did so to a significantly greater extent than junior teachers. Like teachers at the secondary stage, both infant and junior teachers placed greatest weight on 'teaching'; but unlike the secondary teachers they thought their pupils placed greatest weight on 'personality'. As with teachers at the secondary stage, infant and junior teachers appeared to be in conflict chiefly over the opposing emphasis they thought that pupils and headteachers placed on personality.)

The primary schools were classified according to the type of social area they served. Areas were classified as 'middle class' if at least two-thirds of the pupils' parents were in white-collar occupations, as 'working class' if at least two-thirds were in manual occupations, and as 'mixed' if the proportions of white-collar and manual workers were approximately equal.

Teachers, whether men or women, no matter what their age or length of teaching experience, if they were teaching in junior schools serving a predominantly working-class catchment area, were in higher conflict about their role as teachers than their colleagues in schools serving a mixed or mainly middle-class area. A similar tendency, although not reaching an acceptable level of statistical significance, is present among infant school teachers.

In working-class areas the discrepancy between a teacher's ideal conception of his role and his perceived expectations of others increased particularly with regard to the perceived expectations of parents, but also with regard to the perceived expectations of pupils, head and colleagues. This may reflect a confusion of aims

Table 14
Role Conflict and Social Area
(137 Junior School Teachers)

Social Composition of Area	Low Conflict ($P_w < 0.01$)	Medium Conflict ($P_w < 0.05$)	High Conflict ($P_w > 0.05$)
Middle Class	9 (60·0%)	3 (20·0%)	3 (20·0%)
Mixed	17 (33·3%)	9 (17·6%)	25 (49·0%)
Working Class	17 (23·9%)	14 (19·7%)	71 (56·3%)

Chi-square = 10·3 $P < 0.05$

Table 15
Role Conflict and Social Area
(48 Infant School Teachers)

Social Composition of Area	Low to Medium Conflict ($P_w < 0.05 > 0.01$)	High Conflict ($P_w > 0.05$)
Middle Class and Mixed	20 (62·5%)	12 (37·6%)
Working Class	9 (56·3%)	7 (43·7%)

Chi-square = 0·17 N.S.

in schools in working-class areas which disturbs not only teacher–parent relationships but relationships among all members of staff.

The research reported in this chapter pin-points the head-teacher as a major source of conflict for teachers. (Only women teachers in grammar schools perceive the head's expectations as roughly in accord with their own values.) In general the head is seen as placing great emphasis on the teachers' disciplinary abilities when they would place the major emphasis elsewhere. Men teaching in secondary modern schools differed little from their perception of the head's expectations in this matter, but attached far more importance to 'personality' than they thought he did. This does not prove that the direction of the schools in this sample is in fact highly authoritarian but it does indicate that assistant staff often feel that they are judged by their superiors according to criteria which they feel are not of the first importance.

The greater proportion of teachers in high conflict in modern schools compared with grammar schools is not surprising in view of the less certain objectives of the former. Teachers in modern schools were also much more at odds with the perceived expectations of their pupils. The absence of any difference between graduates and non-graduates in modern schools is perhaps more surprising. There was no evidence in this inquiry that intra-role-conflict was any greater among married than unmarried women teachers. It is possible that if 'teacher's role' has been more widely defined to include extra-mural as well as classroom work, some difference might have emerged.

The low level of conflict among mathematics specialists perhaps reflects the prestige and generally agreed importance of mathematics as a school subject. The high levels of conflict among teachers of domestic subjects are more difficult to explain. They are in line with the findings of Rudd and Wiseman that teachers of housecraft have lower levels of job-satisfaction than other teachers.[22] The low status of domestic science as a school subject may also be a source of tension and conflict.

Both men and women in all types of school seem to exist, as it were, as a bridge between the perceived values of the head and the contrary values of their pupils particularly in their evaluation of 'personality' in the teacher's role. In comparison with pupils, headteachers are seen as attaching little importance to friendly, sympathetic and understanding personal relationships; the teachers themselves stand midway in the emphasis they place on these attributes.

The high levels of conflict apparently experienced by teachers in working-class areas need to be more fully explored and understood at a time when special attention is directed – after the Report of the Plowden Committee on Primary Schools – to the needs of 'Educational Priority Areas'. Schools in socially deprived districts are in need not only of more resources but of searching debate on their function and agreement among staff about educational ends and means.

A fuller understanding of teachers' role conflicts is likely to be particularly important in the near future as English education is extensively re-organized and established institutions change their nature. The sharp distinction between grammar schools and secondary modern schools is likely to disappear as Government policy encourages a less conservative educational system. Teachers in grammar schools are likely to develop sharper role conflicts than they show at present. They may be required to teach less able pupils and pursue different educational objectives. They will probably be less confident that their aims coincide with the expectations of their pupils; their low evaluation of 'discipline' may need upward revision.

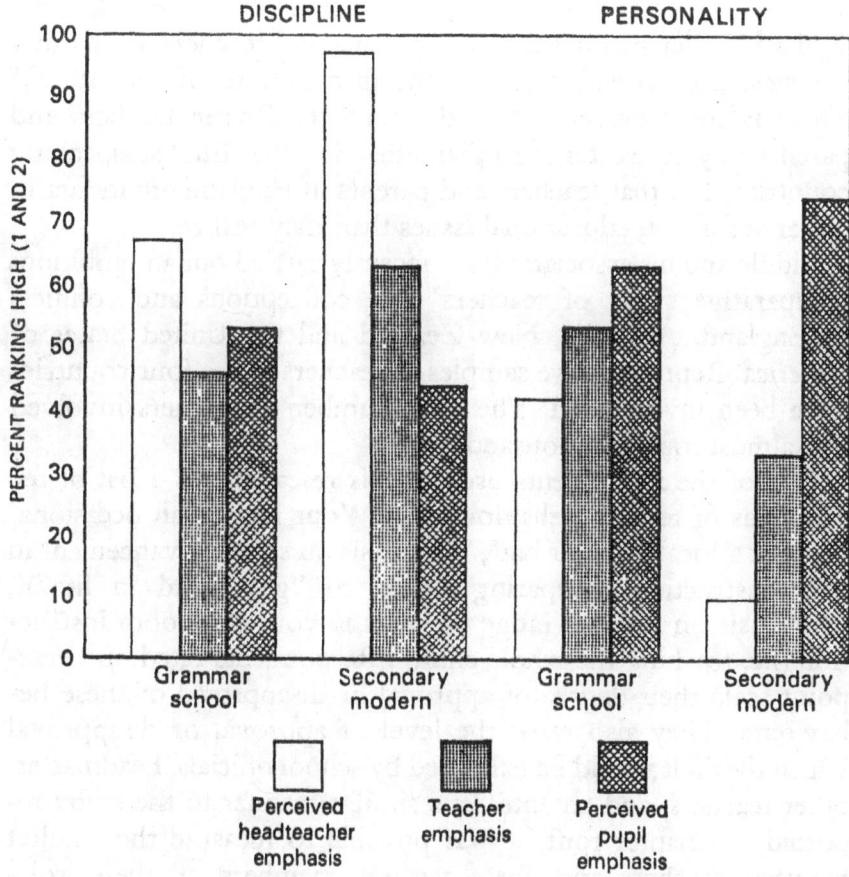

Fig. 3. Female Secondary School Teachers.

This is one of two diagrams. The other of which is to be found on page 51.

Chapter Five
PARENTS VERSUS TEACHERS

Willard Waller maintained that 'parents and teachers are natural enemies, predestined each for the discomfiture of the other'.[1] There is some evidence that the conflict between teachers and parents may be greater in England than in other English-speaking countries; but that teachers and parents in England are in fact in closer accord on educational issues than they realize.

Biddle and his associates have recently carried out an ambitious comparative study of teachers' role conceptions and conflicts in England, Australia, New Zealand and the United States of America. Representative samples of teachers in the four countries have been investigated. The total number of teachers involved was almost fourteen thousand.

One of the instruments used in this research was a list of ten problems of teacher behaviour, e.g. 'Your having an occasional drink at a local hotel or bar', 'Emphasis on social advancement in your instruction (preparing pupils to "get ahead in life")', 'Emphasis on a broad range of goals in your classroom instruction (i.e. teaching the whole child)'. Respondents rated on a five-point scale their degree of approval or disapproval of these behaviours. They also rated the level of approval or disapproval which they felt would be exhibited by school officials, headmaster, other teachers, and parents. In a similar manner to the study reported in Chapter four, it was possible to measure the conflict between teachers and these various members of their 'role-set'.

One of the most striking findings of this research was that conflict between parents and teachers was greater in England than in any of the other countries investigated. 'One striking characteristic of the English responses was the amount of role conflict revealed between teacher respondents and parents. In at least half (of the ten problem areas) greater disparities are revealed between parents and respondents themselves for England than for the other three countries. . . . Thus, our data suggest considerable social distance, or perhaps hostility, between teachers and parents in England.'[2]

Teachers differed markedly from the views they ascribed to parents especially on the two items: 'Emphasis on a broad range of goals in your classroom instruction' and 'Emphasis on social advancement in your instruction'. With regard to the first of these items, teachers in all four countries saw parents attaching less importance than anyone else to breadth of instruction; they themselves attached more importance than they thought was attached by anyone else. (The gap between teacher-emphasis and perceived parent-emphasis was smaller in America than in the other three countries.)

Teachers in all four countries placed comparatively little emphasis on social advancement as an object of instruction; all saw parents as placing the greatest emphasis on this objective. The largest gap between teachers and perceived parental expectations occurred in England; the smallest gap again occurred in America. Teachers in England 'thoroughly disagreed with parents over the emphasis to be given to social advancement'. More accurately, they thoroughly disagreed with what they *thought* was the emphasis that parents gave.

These findings support the conclusions reached by the authors in an inquiry among English teachers which is reported below. The present investigation was concerned with the way the teacher sees his role in relation to the perceived and actual expectations of parents. The inquiry attempted to relate teachers' role conceptions to the type of schools and social area in which they worked; and to discover not only what teachers thought parents expected, but what in fact parents expected.[3]

It has been argued that the teacher's role must become more 'diffuse' at a time when most professional roles are becoming more specialized and specific. 'The diffuse role means diffuse involvement'.[4] Mays has similarly argued that the teacher's role must broaden in scope, embracing even more 'parental' functions and calling for the skills and interests of the social worker. 'The argument then is between the idea of the teacher as a pure inculcator of knowledge and the teacher as a welfare worker. It is not so much that the two interpretations of the teacher's role need be mutually exclusive. The disagreement concerns the degree of emphasis and the amount of time and energy to be devoted to these related aspects of the job.'⁵

The purpose of the inquiry reported in this chapter was to estimate to what extent teachers in different types of school and circumstances saw their roles as 'diffuse' or 'restricted'; what weight they attached to different aspects of their work; what weight they thought parents expected them to give to different educational objectives; and what weight parents did, in fact, attach to these objectives. This study was parallel to the investigation reported in the previous chapter (Chapter Four), using the same schools and teachers.

THE NATURE OF THE INQUIRY

The instrument used was a questionnaire which listed six commonly accepted educational aims. These aims which teachers are seen as pursuing were those frequently mentioned by parents in the interviews reported in Chapter three of this book. The aims were: I Moral Training (the inculcation of values and attitudes, e.g. honesty, kindliness, tolerance, courage); II Instruction in Subjects (imparting information and promoting understanding of a body of knowledge); III Social Training (encouraging politeness, good manners, decency in speech and dress, etc.); IV Education for Family Life (training in human relationships with special reference to attitudes to the opposite sex); V Social Advancement (preparing children to 'get on in life'); and VI Education for Citizenship (developing an understanding of the modern world, etc.).

The teachers involved in this research were asked to rank these objectives as they valued them and also as their experience led them to believe that parents in general, valued them. They were also asked to indicate any objective which they regarded as no concern of theirs and none of their business as teachers. The parents who took part in the inquiry – a sample of 108 parents of primary school children and 129 parents of children at the secondary stage in one of the three local authority areas selected for research – were asked to rank these objectives as they thought they should weigh with the teachers in charge of their children, and to indicate any of the listed objectives which they regarded as none of the teacher's business.

Fifty men and 37 women teaching in the grammar schools completed the schedule, 103 men and 91 women in the modern schools. At the primary stage, 189 teachers completed the schedule, 51 (all women) in the infant schools and 138 (48 men and 90 women) in the junior schools.

The primary schools were classified as denominational and non-denominational; and also according to the type of social area they serve. As described in Chapter four, if two-thirds of the pupils' parents were in white-collar occupations the school was classified as 'middle-class'; if two-thirds were in manual occupations as 'working class'; if the proportions of white-collar and manual workers were roughly equal as 'mixed'.

DIFFUSENESS OF ROLE CONCEPTION AND EXPECTATION

An individual teacher's diffuse or restricted conception of his role was measured by the number of educational objectives he regarded as none of his business. On this estimation grammar school teachers had a more restricted notion of their role than secondary modern school teachers: 9 per cent of the ratings of male grammar school teachers indicated 'no concern of mine', only 3·2 per cent of the ratings by men teaching in modern schools.[6] The corresponding ratings by women in the two types of school were 11 per cent and 4 per cent.[7] The objectives which were rejected were exclusively social, as opposed to moral and intellectual aims.

Primary school teachers stood between grammar and modern school teachers in their restricted view of their role: 8 per cent of their ratings indicated 'no concern'. Like teachers at the secondary stage, the aims they rejected were all social in nature.

Infant school teachers, whether married or single, old or young, with or without much teaching experience, and irrespective of whether they worked in schools serving predominantly upper or lower-class social areas, rejected around the same percentage of all objectives.

Married women teachers in junior schools rejected a significantly higher percentage of objectives than men teachers, single women teachers, and teachers in infant schools[8] (see Table 16). Junior school teachers working in schools serving a predominantly middle-class catchment area have a significantly more restricted role conception than their colleagues in schools serving

Table 16
Restricted or Diffuse Role Conception of Junior and Infant School Teachers According to Sex and Marital Status

Teachers' Sex and Marital Status	Junior Teachers				Infant Teachers			
	N	Max ranks	'No concern'	%	N	Max Ranks	'No concern'	%
Men	51	306	19	6·2				
Single Women	51	306	23	7·5	25	150	12	8·0
Married Women	35	210	46	12·4	22	132	11	8·3
All Women	86	516	49	9·5				
Total	138	328	68	8·2	47	282	23	8·2

Table 17
Teachers' Restricted or Diffuse Role Conception According to Social-Class Area and Denominational Status of School

Type of Area and Denominational Status of School	Junior Teachers				Infant Teachers			
	N	Max Ranks	'No concern'	%	N	Max Ranks	'No concern'	%
Middle Class and Mixed	66	396	42	10·6	32	192	16	8·3
Working Class	72	432	26	6·1	15	90	7	7·8
Denominational	40	240	23	9·6	14	84	6	7·7
Non-denominational	98	588	45	7·6	33	198	17	8·6

working-class districts. They rejected over 10 per cent as against 6 per cent of the objectives.[9] Married women junior school teachers and junior school teachers working in middle-class areas thus exhibited about the same degree of role restriction as teachers in grammar schools.

The 108 parents of primary school children who completed the questionnaire ascribed a significantly wider range of educational objectives to teachers if they were working class than if they were middle class. The opposite was the case with the 129 parents with children in secondary schools: working-class parents ascribed to teachers a comparatively restricted role, particularly with regard to social objectives; middle-class parents now expected a significantly wider range of services from teachers.

Table 18
Ascription of Diffuse or Restricted Role to Teachers by Parents

	Percentage of ratings indicating objectives of no concern to teachers			
	'Social Class' (Registrar-General)			
	I–II	III Non-manual	III Manual	IV–V
Parents of Primary Children. N: 108	11·8	9·7	6·3	2·8
Parents of Secondary Children. N: 129	1·6	5·2	10·6	9·2

TEACHERS' ROLE CONCEPTION, PERCEIVED EXPECTATIONS OF PARENTS, AND ACTUAL EXPECTATIONS OF PARENTS

Teachers in all types of school saw their work primarily in intellectual and moral terms, placing greatest weight on instruction in subjects and moral training. They placed comparatively little emphasis on social objectives in general, and least of all on 'social advancement' in particular. In no type of school were teachers prepared to see themselves primarily as agents of social mobility. They saw parents as being comparatively indifferent to moral and social training, but placing great weight on instruction and on social advancement. In fact, the parents in general emphasized the same objectives as teachers: moral training and instruction in subjects; and, like teachers, gave comparatively little weight to 'social advancement' (although there were significant social-class differences in this regard).

There were no significant differences between the emphases of junior and infant teachers. Both gave greatest weight to moral training and least to social advancement; instruction in subjects and social training were given roughly equal weight after moral training.

Among teachers at the secondary stage, as at the primary, moral training took pride of place over 'instruction' for all except men teaching in grammar schools, who seem to perceive their job primarily in intellectual terms. As with primary school teachers, 'social advancement' came last except for women teachers in modern schools who, rather curiously, gave least emphasis to 'education for family life'.

Society and the Teacher's Role

Table 19
Median Rank Order of Teachers' Aims
(Order ascribed to parents by teachers in brackets)

	Moral Training	Instruction	Social Training	Family Life	Social Advance	Citizenship
Grammar School Men	2 (3)	1 (1)	4 (4)	5 (6)	6 (2)	3 (5)
Grammar School Women	1 (5)	2 (1)	5 (3)	4 (4)	6 (2)	3 (6)
Modern School Men	1 (3)	2 (1)	3 (4)	5 (6)	6 (2)	4 (5)
Modern School Women	1 (3)	1 (1)	3 (4)	6 (5)	5 (2)	4 (5)
Actual parents' ranks	1	2	4	6	5	3
Junior Teachers	1 (4)	2 (1)	3 (3)	5 (6)	5 (2)	4 (5)
Infant Teachers	1 (3)	2 (1)	2 (4)	4 (6)	5 (2)	3 (5)
Actual parents' ranks	2	1	4	6	5	3

Some statistically significant differences emerged between the order of priorities found among modern school and grammar school teachers. Forty-two per cent of men teaching in modern schools ranked 'social training' first or second, only 20 per cent of men teaching in grammar schools did so.[10] Similarly, with regard to moral training: 74 per cent of modern school teachers gave it a high rating, only 60 per cent of male grammar school teachers did so.[11] Eighty-six per cent of male grammar school teachers rated 'instruction' first or second compared with 63 per cent in the modern schools.

Male grammar school teachers of non-academic subjects – woodwork, metalwork, religious instruction, art and music – gave no less weight to 'instruction' as their primary goal than teachers of academic subjects. Women teachers in the two types of school differed significantly in only one respect – in the greater emphasis which secondary modern school teachers placed on social training as an educational aim. Only 5·6 per cent of women teaching in grammar schools ranked this objective high but a third of the women teachers in modern schools did so.[12]

The following chart shows the educational priorities of all the teachers at the secondary stage compared with the priorities they ascribed to parents and with the priorities which were, in fact, found among the sample of parents of secondary school children. (There were 281 teachers and 129 parents.)

Parents like teachers, in fact, gave greatest weight to moral

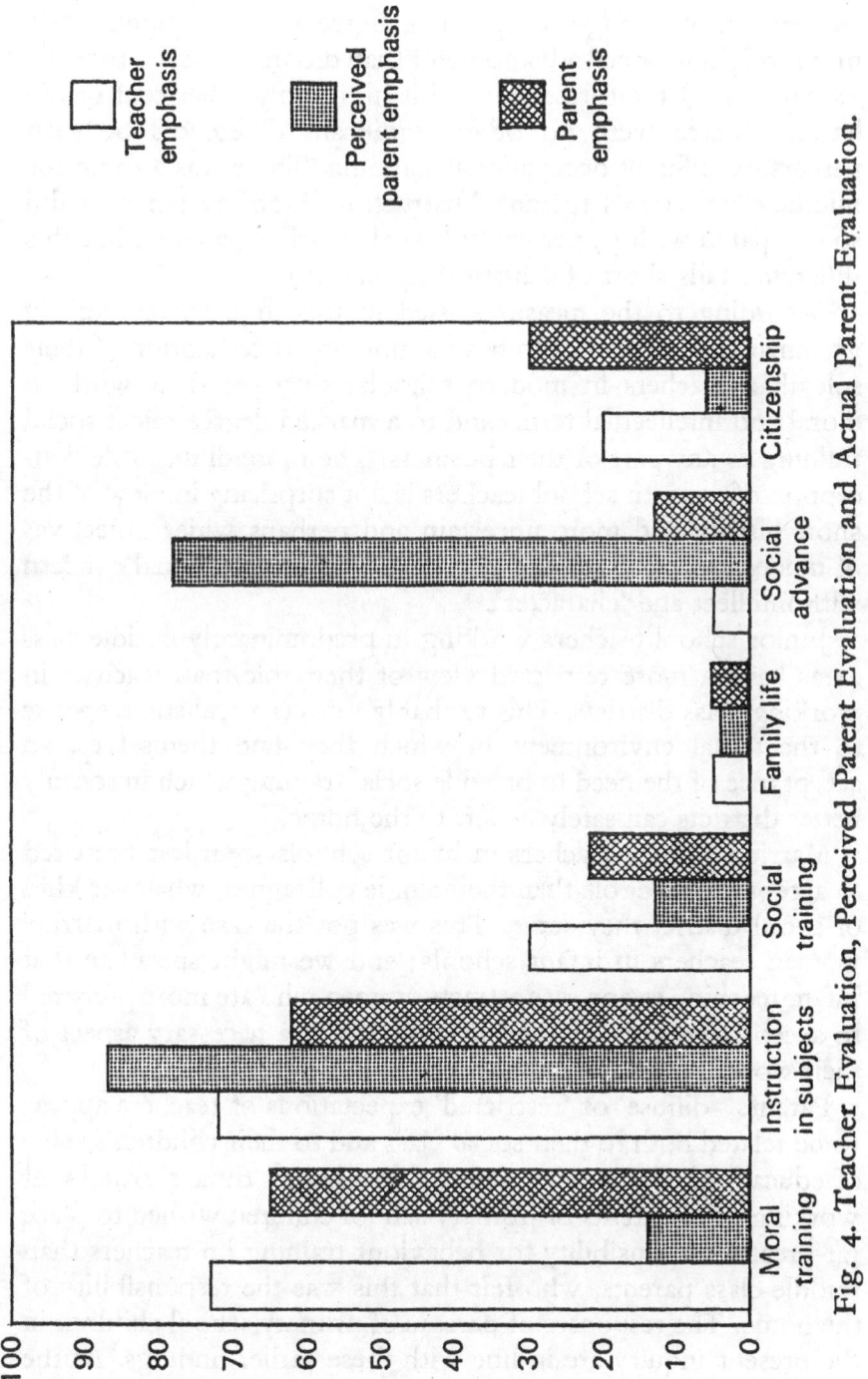

Fig. 4. Teacher Evaluation, Perceived Parent Evaluation and Actual Parent Evaluation.

training and instruction and comparatively little to social advancement. Working-class parents, however, gave significantly more weight to social advancement than did middle-class parents: 18 per cent of the former ranked it high, only 2 per cent of the latter.[13] There were no other significant differences between parents of different occupational standing. There was a trend for middle-class parents to rank 'instruction' high (72 per cent did so compared with 59 per cent of working-class parents), but this difference falls short of statistical significance.

According to the measures used in this inquiry, teachers in grammar schools appear to have a more restricted notion of their role than teachers in modern schools: they see their work in moral and intellectual terms and to a marked degree reject social training as any part of their business. The more diffuse role conception of modern school teachers is not surprising in view of the short history and more uncertain and perhaps wider objectives of modern schools, and the grammar school's traditional concern with intellect and 'character'.

Junior school teachers working in predominantly middle-class areas have a more restricted view of their role than teachers in working-class districts. This probably reflects a realistic response to the social environment in which they find themselves, an acceptance of the need to provide social training which in socially better districts can safely be left to the home.

Married women teachers in junior schools seem less prepared to accept a diffuse role than their single colleagues, whatever kind of social district they serve. This was not the case with married women teachers in infant schools; and we might speculate that infant teaching in any case attracts women who are more prepared to accept a general 'mothering' function as a necessary aspect of their work.

Parents' 'diffuse' or 'restricted' expectations of teachers appear to be related both to their social class and to their children's stage of education. The inquiry reported in Chapter three showed that working-class parents of primary school children wished to place far greater responsibility for behaviour-training on teachers than middle-class parents, who felt that this was the responsibility of the home. The responses of parents of primary school children in the present inquiry are in line with these earlier findings. At the secondary school stage it seems to be middle-class parents who would make the widest and most general demands on teachers (except that working-class parents have stronger expectations with regard to 'social advancement'). Working-class parents perhaps look particularly to the school as an ally when their children are young, vulnerable and exposed to an inauspicious local social environment.

Teachers in all types of school see their role in moral and intellectual terms and are comparatively indifferent to the more specifically social aims of education. Secondary modern school teachers placed more weight on social objectives than their grammar school colleagues, but nevertheless, placed much greater emphasis on 'instruction in school subjects'. In emphasizing 'instruction' teachers were in line with what they thought parents expected and with what parents in fact expected.

But the area of discrepancy between teachers' aims and what they imagine to be parents' is still very large. On the whole, teachers take an unflattering view of parents (and their own aims are remarkably idealistic), seeing them as indifferent to moral training but very concerned with social advancement. In fact, parents were substantially in agreement with teachers. The area of (unnecessary) tension might be considerably reduced if parents and teachers established more effective means of communication.

Chapter Six
PROBLEMS OF STATUS AND ROLE

Role problems are closely connected with problems of status.[1] Many teachers today are in difficulties not because they occupy statuses which are too low, but which are too high. During the nineteen-sixties two processes have brought rapid and unexpected status improvement for many people engaged in education: one is the swift expansion of the education service particularly at its highest levels; the other is the upgrading of many institutions – secondary modern to high or comprehensive schools, colleges of advanced technology to universities, technical or teacher-training colleges to institutions engaged in degree-level work. Some academic subjects have also expanded with remarkable rapidity and have also improved their status. In consequence large numbers of teachers find themselves, often to their astonishment, and even to their dismay, in positions to which they had never aspired. Their problem is to validate their occupation of statuses for which they have no recognized title or qualification.[2]

In the past few years teachers on a large scale have been involved in migrations between different status areas of the educational service. A great deal of this migration has been involuntary – it has occurred by suction or by decree. When secondary or higher education has been 're-organized', teachers have found themselves overnight in positions which they had never sought, often involving unfamiliar tasks and obligations. Men who were technical teachers have found themselves university lecturers with an obligation to engage in research; headmasters appointed ten years previously to small secondary schools have found themselves presiding over large comprehensive schools with (some) highly qualified staff and a commitment to advanced academic study. Those who have been so unexpectedly elevated have the problem of learning and justifying their new role; those who have failed to receive such elevation are thrown into a state of status panic. When promotion is unusually common (and often arbitrary), the non-promoted are more inclined to feel resentful of their lot.

Apart from involuntary migration by decree, the migration of teachers to new statuses has been occurring by a kind of suction as areas of educational activity expand and draw incumbents into the new role positions available. Never were so many people sucked into positions of importance. Some of the unintended consequences of this process are worth close scrutiny.

In particular the expansion of higher education has created many new jobs in a very short time. There has been an especially rapid expansion of departments of sociology and education in our universities and colleges of education. People with appropriate qualities and qualifications have not always been available. We have witnessed over the past four or five years a curious spectacle of recruitment by social capilliarity. People have been sucked into the new jobs from a variety of fields by what has sometimes seemed an almost random process. They have been drawn across previously impenetrable boundaries because the jobs happen to be there.

This is not necessarily an undesirable process. But it has given rise to an acute condition of 'status incongruence' – and in general this is *not* a desirable state of affairs. Status incongruence occurs when an individual exhibits two or more discrepant status factors, for example, when one of Her Majesty's Inspectors of Schools speaks with a Cockney accent; when a senior executive is twenty years of age; when a university professor hasn't got a university degree; when a grammar school headmaster lives in a council house. When many members of a social system have incongruent statuses, the functioning of the system is likely to be impaired.

Status incongruence is disturbing because people expect certain linkages between status factors. A good honours degree is expected to go hand-in-hand with a grammar school, rather than a primary school, appointment; an Oxbridge degree may be associated with posts in independent schools. Incongruent people – like doctors of philosophy in secondary modern schools – are punished for their incongruence. If it is within their power they will try to remedy their inferior characteristics.

We have had recently a proliferation of incongruent people. Many are urgently attempting to remedy their inferior characteristics. And so we have the rather odd situation that people are trying to obtain university degrees not in order to get jobs, but because they have got jobs. Nongraduates who are lecturers (or even senior or principal lecturers) in colleges of education are desperate to get the degree of M.Ed. Higher degrees in education are becoming means of legitimizing promotion already obtained; they are means of validating positions already held. (And in the circumstances it is probably highly desirable that we should make these degrees more widely available as remedies for status incongruence.)

All this matters because there is good evidence that organizations in which average status congruence is low, are not very happy places.[3] They are not very attractive to their members; there is a high turnover rate, if jobs are available elsewhere. Schools with incongruent headmasters and other senior teachers – people who have perhaps little relevant experience and no university degree – tend to be institutions riven by resentments. The redrawing of boundaries around educational subsystems has even wider ramifications than administrators suppose.

Changes in the nature and prestige of academic subjects are also presenting teachers with problems of status and role. Academic subjects have become highly organized social systems with heavily defended boundaries. Behind these boundaries their members are arrayed in hierarchical formation: they have assumed many of the characteristics of powerful bureaucracies, with strong national and regional associations. They campaign to improve their academic status relative to other subjects: they publish justifications for their existence, ideologies and utopias, in the form of 'philosophies' of the subject. Their unvalidated claims to potency as instruments of education constitute 'philosophy and principles of education' courses in colleges of education. If they are new subjects their 'philosophies' are unusually portentous; if they are old and venerable they can maintain their position by perpetuating heroic myths.

These increasingly powerful organizations maintain their boundaries and in doing so resist curriculum change – particularly when this involves the amalgamation of subjects. 'Subjects' provide their members not only with a livelihood, but with a sense of identity. While curriculum change may not often threaten a member's livelihood, it frequently threatens his sense of identity.

An academic subject may afford safe anchorage for a teacher's self concept.

When boundaries between different subjects are removed or re-drawn, their practitioners must learn new roles. Or they may cling obstinately to their former roles and modes of operation, however inappropriate in the changed circumstances, particularly if they feel their former status has been undermined. Teachers of physics who find themselves teachers of general science, teachers of history or geography who find themselves teachers of social studies, may cling to and even exaggerate their former modes of teaching and general intellectual style, often with grotesque consequences.

This process has been closely examined by Ben-David in connection with the development of academic subjects in the nineteenth century. Ben-David has investigated the 'role-hybridization' which occurs when men cross the boundary from one academic subject to another. He has shown how the very conservatism of 'role-hybrids' can be a source of intellectual innovation and advance. He has looked at the rise of experimental psychology in nineteenth-century Germany in these terms.[4] Physiologists were drawn (for promotion) to the relatively low status field of philosophy; by continuing to behave as physiologists and to apply the methods of physiology to philosophy, they created experimental psychology. One doubts whether the conservatism of role-hybrids is always as productive of exciting innovation. University Departments of Education are staffed by role-hybrids. The outcome has not, perhaps, been quite as fruitful.

Subjects have tended to change their modes of operation (and their ideologies) to promote or justify an enhanced academic status. In theory all subjects of the curriculum have an equal standing today. Teachers in all subject areas receive the same pay; there is no formal differentiation of status among teachers according to the subjects they teach. But in fact different subjects enjoy different levels of prestige: their status appears to be related in some measure to the kind of role performance and general teaching style expected of their practitioners.

EDUCATION AND TRAINING

Within the profession of teaching there are wide variations of function according to one's subject and the age and ability of one's pupils. In the past a broad distinction has been made between trainers and instructors on the one hand, and teachers, tutors, educators and lecturers on the other. The latter have enjoyed a higher status (and often higher pay) than the former: their role has been seen as less constricted, more 'liberal', more concerned with personal relationships and the development of personality. Trainers and instructors have been seen as imparting more or less mechanical skills and uncontroverted fact by rule-of-thumb techniques; their job could be done without deep personal involvement of commitment; their essential method has been drill and repetition, with little scope for the free ranging intelligence and independence of mind.[5]

Vocational education, which demands expertness in the application of tried and tested techniques, is still seen by many as the realm of the trainer or instructor; 'liberal education', which the grammar schools and universities claim to provide, as the realm of the teacher and educator. This is a distinction of status as well as of role: 'training' and 'instructing' carry quite clear derogatory implications. The distinction is often made in such terms as these: 'The essential task of technological institutions is to equip their students to cope with the known. Our task in the universities is to encourage that critical temper, which alone will enable its possessor to cope with the unknown.'[6]

There can be no doubt that these different roles within teaching are still sharply distinguished by many and connote marked differences of status. Yet official policy and administrative regulation have made a determined effort over the past quarter of a century to remove these distinctions, particularly in the maintained secondary schools. Whereas those teachers who might be classified as instructors were formerly on lower salary scales, all qualified teachers, whatever their subject specialism, now enjoy the same basic salary. Changes of nomenclature have been made to assist these developments. Cookery and needlework instructors have become teachers of domestic science; religious instruction has more recently become religious education; drill instructors have evolved into physical education teachers (except in some of our public schools, where they retain their noncommissioned rank and tenuous relationship with the staff room). New claims have been made for the subjects which these specialists profess: they are not simply an organized body of skills and techniques

Problems of Status and Role

which are learned through practice, repetition and drill; they are vehicles for the development of personality in particular and valuable directions. The woodwork teacher has taught more than the mortise and tenon: in placing his pupils in an effective and creative relationship with their material environment he has shaped their personalities.

The teacher training colleges (in England and Wales) suffered until recently from their name. Their training function depressed their status in relation to the universities. The former 'Training Departments' in the universities changed their name earlier: they were re-styled 'Departments of Education'. The emphasis in both types of institution has changed from teacher-training to teacher-education, to the preparation of mature personalities for difficult and demanding social and professional roles, for meeting human problems with intelligence, sensitivity and insight rather than practised routines.

And yet it is probably true that trainers of teachers, whether inside or outside the universities, are seen by the majority of their students, their ex-students now teaching in the schools, and by their academic colleagues, to approximate to trainers of horses and athletes. Their role still suffers from the ambiguities which cookery instructresses have done much to transcend. Indeed the graduate student of education tends to demand (and to some extent to enforce) this more constricted role upon his mentors: he insists on instruction in the 'rules' of teaching; he asks for the pre-packaged answer to the human and pedagogical situations of the classroom. He resents the suggestion that what he still may need is 'education': the personal development which will enable him to meet with flexibility and intelligent improvisation, with an experimental outlook and a capacity to tolerate uncertainty and novelty, the unprecedented human situations with which he is daily confronted.

There is a case for equipping him more completely with techniques of a different kind – with the diagnostic skills of the psychologist; but this is a different issue (which will be taken up again in the concluding chapter). The assumptions of the days when the Master of Method drilled intending teachers from an instructor's manual are no longer valid (if ever they were). The 'normal' colleges no longer imagine themselves guardians of established teaching 'norms' which they transmit to successive generations of students. They see their job as indistinguishable from that often ascribed to the universities: enabling their students 'to cope with the unknown'.

CONNOTATIONS OF INFERIORITY

In order to discover to what extent practising teachers still distinguish between the roles of different subject specialists, and the extent to which these distinctions are associated with differences in status, the authors directed a limited inquiry among the teachers of seven randomly selected Midland schools. Three primary schools, two secondary modern schools and two grammar schools collaborated. There was, however, considerable resistance to the inquiry, particularly among the male teachers in the grammar schools; and the questionnaire which was used was completed by only 55 per cent of the sample. (It was returned by 42 primary school teachers, 26 grammar school teachers, and 48 modern school teachers.) An inquiry into teachers' status and role clearly touched an extremely sensitive area and provoked the hostility of a sizeable minority of the teachers who were approached.

A simple questionnaire was prepared which listed 10 subject specialists or teachers in particular types of institution. The subjects were asked to rank these in order of the prestige and professional standing which, in their view, they enjoyed. They were also asked to indicate what they considered was the major emphasis in the performance of each of the jobs – 'Teaching', 'Training', 'Instructing' or 'Lecturing'. No definition was given of these four functions: the intention was to see whether an agreed distinction existed nevertheless in the minds of a representative body of practising teachers.

The 10 jobs listed were: 1. Teacher of Modern Languages, 2. Infant School Teacher, 3. Woodwork/Domestic Science Teacher, 4. Sixth-form Mathematics Teacher, 5. Secondary Modern School Teacher of General Subjects, 6. Religious Education Teacher, 7. University Teacher, 8. Teacher of Commercial Subjects, 9. Physical Education Teacher, 10. Junior School Teacher. These were ranked by 117 teachers and classified by 116.

In neither the ranking nor the classification of these 10 jobs were there differences between men and women teachers or between teachers in different types of school – except that women teachers in primary schools tended to rank 'Infant School Teacher' higher than the other subjects. (42·3 per cent ranked Infant School Teacher 1–5, only 13·3 per cent of the other teachers did so.)[7] There was no tendency for teachers in any other type of school to differ from other subjects in ranking a teacher in that type of school. Indeed, the agreement in the ranking and classification is one of the most striking features of the inquiry. The results for all 117 teachers who completed the questionnaire are therefore pooled in the tables which follow.

'University Teacher' was accorded the highest rank with the greatest measure of unanimity among the 'judges' (mean rank 1·3, quartile deviation: $Q = 0·0$). 89·6 per cent ranked him first, 93·1 per cent first or second. 'Infant School Teacher' obtained the lowest average rank, but there was more disagreement about the ranking ($Q = 2·0$). The median rank was 9 and the mean rank 7·7. 56·4 per cent ranked her 9 or 10; but 19 per cent ranked her 1 to 5.

There was general agreement in according 'Sixth-form Teacher of Mathematics' and 'Teacher of Modern Languages' high status: distinctly inferior to the university teacher, but distinctly superior to the secondary modern school teacher, who ranked next below them. Specialists in religious education, commercial subjects, woodwork, domestic science and physical education were bunched together in a lower-intermediate position; and there was

Table 20
Prestige Ranking of Teachers

Type of Institution	Teacher	Mean Rank	Quartile Deviation
University	University Teacher	1·3	0·0
Grammar School	Sixth-form Mathematics	2·5	0·0
	Modern Languages	3·5	0·0
Modern School	General Subjects	5·4	1·5
Grammar, Modern or Technical	Religious Education	6·3	2·0
	Commercial Subjects	6·3	2·0
	Woodwork/Domestic Science	6·4	1·5
	Physical Education	6·5	1·5
Junior School	Junior School Teacher	6·7	2·0
Infant School	Infant Teacher	7·7	2·0

more disagreement in the rankings. 'Junior School Teacher' and 'Infant School Teacher' obtained the next-but-lowest and the lowest ranks respectively.

There was substantial agreement over the major function ascribed to the listed teachers. Agreement was particularly high for university teacher, secondary modern school teacher of general subjects, teacher of modern languages, teachers of physical education, woodwork and domestic science. The greatest measure of disagreement was found for teachers of religious education and commercial subjects. 22·4 per cent categorized the teacher of R.E. as an 'instructor', perhaps because he is still perceived to have a catechetical function, or to be an instructor in morals; 48·3 per cent classified the teacher of commercial subjects as an instructor. A sharp distinction emerged between infant school teacher and junior school teacher: the former was seen very largely as a 'trainer', the latter as a 'teacher'.

Table 21
Function of Teachers as Seen by 116 Teachers
(Arranged in order of prestige ranking)

	Teacher	Trainer	Instructor	Lecturer
University teacher	1·8	0·8	0·8	96·6
Sixth-form mathematics teacher	56·2	0·8	7·7	38·9
Modern languages teacher	88·8	0·8	6·9	3·5
General subjects, modern school	92·2	4·3	3·5	0·0
R.E. teacher	51·8	10·4	22·4	15·4
Commercial subjects	27·6	21·5	48·3	2·6
Woodwork/Domestic Science	9·5	31·9	58·6	0·0
P.E. teacher	6·9	57·8	34·5	0·8
Junior school teacher	90·5	7·7	1·8	0·0
Infant school teacher	39·6	56·9	3·5	0·0

The status of a teacher is clearly determined not only by his subject specialism and the mode of operation which this involves, but by the standing of the institution in which he works. A 'teacher' in general has higher prestige than an 'instructor' or 'trainer', but not if he or she works in an institution which carries low status. Thus the teacher of modern languages is seen essentially as a 'teacher'; he is commonly found in grammar schools;

Problems of Status and Role

and these two circumstances assure him high prestige. The junior school teacher (unlike the infant school teacher) is also seen as essentially a 'teacher'; but the standing of junior schools depresses his status below that of 'instructors' in secondary schools.

Teachers of religious education, woodwork, domestic science and physical education (and perhaps commercial subjects) are found equally in grammar and modern schools. Their intermediate rank appears to be determined by their 'trainer-instructor' function, which places them below teachers proper, and by the institutions they serve, which place them above the 'teacher' in the junior school.

There was no apparent tendency for the function of 'lecturing' to confer a higher (or lower) status than the function of teaching – although it might be regarded as a more restricted role with a greater degree of disengagement from personal relationships and pastoral responsibilities. 38·9 per cent categorized the sixth-form teacher of mathematics as a 'lecturer'; but there was no tendency for those who so classified him to rank him differently from those who categorized him as a teacher. (80·9 per cent of those classifying him 'teacher' ranked him 1 or 2, but so did 84·8 per cent of

Table 22
Rank and Function

Median Rank	Teacher	Combined Instructor-Trainer Rating (per cent)	Perceived Major Function (per cent)
1	University teacher	1·6	Lecturer (96·6)
2	Sixth-form Mathematics	8·5	Teacher-lecturer (91·5)
3	Modern languages	7·7	Teacher (88·8)
5	General Subjects (Modern School)	7·8	Teacher (92·2)
6	Religious Education	32·8	Teacher-instructor-lecturer (89·6)
6	Commercial Subjects	69·8	Instructor-teacher (75·9)
6	Woodwork/Domestic Science	90·5	Instructor-trainer (90·5)
7	Physical Education	92·3	Trainer-instructor (90·5)
7	Junior School Teacher	9·5	Teacher (90·5)
9	Infant School Teacher	60·4	Trainer-teacher (96·5)

those who classified him 'lecturer'.) The high status of the university lecturer would appear to derive from the high standing of the institution which employs him and the level of work in which he is engaged, rather than from his method of operation.

We have seen in the post-war history of secondary education how difficult it is to establish parity of esteem among teachers by decree. It is no less difficult to achieve equality of status by changes of name. Status and role are intimately linked. If the status of teachers of different subjects in different institutions is to be comparable, it is necessary that their roles be demonstrably similar. Teachers of domestic science are likely to enjoy the same status as teachers of mathematics only when domestic science is seen to have been clearly re-interpreted as a humane education (perhaps drawing deeply on sociology, anthropology and literature) for sensitive and intelligent as well as technically competent handling of a household's socio-technical procedures and problems.

Chapter Seven
TEACHERS AND CLIENTS

Facts cannot solve problems of right but they can help in their elucidation. This book has been primarily concerned to present empirical research into the teacher's role in contemporary English society. In conclusion we shall briefly consider not what the teacher's role is but what it ought to be.

How free should the teacher be to determine what he teaches and the range of his services? During the first half of the twentieth century the autonomy of the teacher has reached – and now perhaps has passed – its high-water mark. He decides (perhaps in consultation with his immediate colleagues at his school) the content of the curriculum; the human values he presents to his pupils; the very scope of his duties. He is aware of pressures both official and unofficial to teach this or that, to confront his pupils with a particular emphasis in social and personal morality, to take upon himself responsibilities for welfare and social training which were formerly the province of home and church. Examination regulations, the reports of inspectors, the demands of parents, all modify his behaviour to some extent; but he is under no legal compulsion to accommodate himself to these pressures; he is free to respond, or not to respond, as he thinks fit. He is particularly jealous of his freedom from both ministerial and parental 'interference' with regard to the curriculum; his resistance to 'dinner-duty' symbolizes his determination to exclude the tasks of social welfare from his role.

In fact the teacher in the maintained schools insists on a special, even a privileged, position among professional workers in contemporary Britain. He claims the right to disregard his client which no other professional worker enjoys. Unlike the lawyer or the architect he is the arbiter of ends as well as the expert in means. The basis of this position in moral and social philosophy is far from clear. He claims far more than pedagogical skills and a command of educational technology which he places at the service of his clients: he chooses the ends to which they shall be employed. He does not accept from his clients instructions to produce, as far as his material permits, this or that kind of human being; he uses his skills to produce the kinds of human being that he in his wisdom sees fit to produce. (On the other hand, he has no right, which other professional men enjoy, to refuse his services to a client of whose objectives he disapproves. This is one of (the many) moral issues raised by the introduction of compulsory education which we have not yet as a society faced or even formulated.)

The right of teachers to determine the ends of education and to disregard entirely the will of their clients seemed self-evident a century or even half a century ago when their work was principally among the working classes. The working classes were virtually synonymous with the 'criminal classes' and teachers had the obvious and self-justifying task of civilizing them. Their ends had the self-evident validity of the Victorian missionary's in Africa. It was obvious that the teacher's (often painfully acquired) middle-class habits, values and skills should displace as far as possible those of his working-class pupils. The moral superiority of his standards required no demonstration.

But we are probably in error in treating the majority of parents – even working-class parents – in mid-twentieth-century Britain as near-criminals, irresponsible and ill-informed. They are the heirs of a century of popular schooling and massive educational and social endeavour. Even lower working-class parents who were interviewed in the inquiries reported above were frequently keenly interested, well informed and extremely thoughtful in their attitudes to education; but often they were neither sufficiently articulate nor socially competent to seek out the schoolmaster and present their views.

Anthropologists, sociologists and men of letters have shewn us often unsuspected values in the working-class 'subculture': middle-class thrift, sobriety, self-reliance and foresight are no longer so obviously preferable to spontaneity, generosity and the ethic of reciprocity: verbal fluency to manual skills and physical power and dexterity. The criminality of the working classes, though it may more often receive official penalties, is probably neither more extensive nor more reprehensible than the criminality of the suburban middle classes.

It would be dangerous, however, to ascribe to such entities as 'subcultures' (or even whole cultures) the right to determine the teacher's role: the right to self-preservation and self-perpetuation with the teacher simply the instrument to this end. The autonomy of subcultures is more inimical to the rights of pupils than the autonomy of teachers. They are perpetuated only by rearing those who are born into them in conformity with the established pattern of life. The subculture can become a prison with the teacher as gaoler.

Although he attempted to provide safeguards against such an education for conformity, it was essentially as the agent of a culture (or subculture) that the late Sir Fred Clarke saw the work of the teacher. Clarke equated Durkheim's (quite ethically neutral) 'social facts' and the (equally neutral) 'culture' of the anthropologists with Rousseau's 'General Will' and thus invested them with a moral imperative:[1] a culture had a *right* to impose itself upon its members, upon each uprising generation, and in Western cultures it employed special agents, the teachers, to this end. The latter had no room for manoeuvre; they had a specific brief. Clarke felt he had made sufficient concession to traditional liberal thought by requiring that, while the teacher aimed at 'the production of a given citizen type':[2] he should also, somehow, educate for 'growth beyond the type'.

> It is the first business of education to induce such conformity in terms of the culture in which the child will grow up. No amount of indiscriminate denouncing of so-called 'indoctrination' can change the necessities of the process by which we become civilized human beings. A child cannot even learn his mother-tongue without being indoctrinated.[3]

The teacher (along with all the other agencies of the so-called 'educative society') is thus essentially the servant of the culture in which he finds himself, 'for whatever else education may mean, it must mean primarily the self-perpetuation of an accepted culture – a culture which is the life of a determinate society'.[4] Clarke never squarely faced the problem of 'subcultures' – but it is difficult to see how he could deny them rights which he accorded to cultures; and in the official reports on the curriculum which he inspired as chairman of the Central Advisory Council for Education, subcultural values and traditions are tenderly regarded: 'A school is always, wherever and whatever it is, part of a social unit, a context, an environment: and it cannot escape the consequences of its geographical situation'.[5] The local world should provide the core of the school's curriculum, the inspiration and direction of the teacher's activities.

It was in discussion of education in the more clearly delineated subculture of the Welsh community that the pressure of Durkheim's 'social facts' was seen to be not only inescapable as a matter of fact, but obligatory as a matter of right:

> all education implies community and some degree of conformity. If the needs of the child are rightly understood, we must insist that any view of personality is defective which does not see the individual as a member of a community and that therefore education will only be truly child-centred when it recognizes that it must in some sort conform to something that is 'external' to the child, namely a pattern of life and ideals cherished by the community, in other words to a culture.[6]

On such a view the role of the teacher is not to dictate to or to disregard the community in which he works, far less to transform it, but to mirror its dominant values and perpetuate them. This philosophy has not been either logically or rigorously applied in Britain: it has had some effect on the curriculum; and perhaps on the attitudes of education committees who, particularly when appointing junior school headmasters, have encouraged them to live in and share the life of the community they serve. But in general the teacher in Britain has remained obstinately impervious to sociology; he has triumphed over social anthropology.

The American teacher has had less success against the deep-rooted political radicalism of his society, which insists that its teachers, like its congressmen, shall recognize the sovereignty of the people. In Britain the people is not sovereign; and perhaps for this reason both teachers and parliamentarians have greater latitude, more freedom of manoeuvre. Of course they can be brought to book, but their work is not defined in detail by a mandate from the people whom they serve. Weldon has distinguished between 'radical democracy' as practised in America and 'individualist democracy' as practised in Britain; the former 'exalts the rights of man but has very little confidence in his competence . . . laws rather than individual judgments control action'.[7] This distinction may perhaps afford a clue to the contrast between the roles of the American and the English teacher: the former is closely bound by the regulations and the folkways of his society; the latter claims an independence of thought and action, a right to exercise private judgment.

In America it is the job of the teacher to mirror and perpetuate his local world; he is seen as 'the instrument of the popular will rather than as the interpreter of knowledge':[8]

> the teacher is firmly regarded as the agent of the local community which she serves. As such she is 'hired' – the word itself is significant – not infrequently for a year at a time, and is required to comply in not a few cases with rigid conventions governing her off-duty life. These may include, in rural areas (although her school duties are wholly secular), church attendance and Sunday school teaching, besides abstinence from alcohol and tobacco. Similar, though less passively accepted, restraints are imposed on men teachers.[9]

Research on the teacher's role-conflicts in America has shewn how the community, no less than the school administrator, may dictate classroom content and procedures in direct opposition to the teacher's best professional judgment.[10] In his *Constraint and Variety in American Education* David Riesman maintains that 'the teacher is required today to be a "good guy", warm and friendly, not too eccentrically dedicated to interests in which the community cannot share . . .' The influence of parents on the curriculum becomes ever greater as more and more parents are themselves high-school graduates.

The American situation is 'democratic' in the sense that education expresses the will of the people; the English situation is 'democratic' in the sense that it offers the maximum opportunity to children to escape their local world: the former offers justice to parents, the latter justice to children.

But it could in Britain be offered more abundantly. Justice requires the elimination of parents from direct involvement in education and the disregard by teachers of local community traditions and values. Equality of educational opportunity is possible only when parents have been equalized – only thus can the child be liberated from the limitations of family and neighbourhood. But parents have their rights: the right to choose the teachers they want, and to change them; to enter the same contractual relationship with teachers as they might with a surgeon for their child, whilst forbearing to take any part in the actual surgery. Neither subservience to local communities and 'subcultures' nor arrogant disdain of their clients seems necessary for the teacher in a well-ordered and just society.

This is in fact what we find in the private sector of education. The public schools offer a service freely chosen by the client from a wide range of possibilities; the parent is a party to at least an implicit contract to produce the type of person for which the school is perhaps famous and which may even be specified in some detail in the prospectus. The teacher in the maintained secondary modern or grammar school aims to produce persons of a kind which he alone has judged desirable: in the former type of institution he is not even constrained by any particular tradition. While there are fairly obvious limits to the teacher's freedom to be wildly eccentric or out of line with contemporary values and morality, he claims and in fact exercises a considerable measure of autonomy. (He will decide, for instance, in his method of teaching and school organization, whether he is producing human beings who are essentially competitive or co-operative.) The client has little option but to accept the roles which teachers in the maintained schools available to his children ascribe to themselves.

The clients who support the roles which teachers have taken upon themselves in fee-paying boarding (and day) schools enjoy the rights which a man enjoys who employs an architect or lawyer. And the teachers in such institutions are as much the servants of their clients as are other professional men. They have joined a school whose objectives they know, approve, and wish to further. Rugby, Abbotsholme, Winchester, Dartington Hall, Sedbergh, Wellington, Rossall, Summerhill, Lancing or Gordonstoun – all offer a different service: they aim, within the limits of the material they are given and the power of human institutions and pedagogical skills, to fashion particular kinds of people. The client chooses, usually in the light of the aptitudes and abilities of his child which have been professionally assessed over the years in a preparatory school, what kind of human being he wants produced, where the main emphasis should lie – on a developed social conscience, on a sensitivity to the arts and personal relationships, on courage or intellect, on 'all-round development', even on the 'qualities of leadership'. The teacher is no more infallible than the surgeon; but in these institutions he does not claim the right to prescribe for humanity: he offers a particular brand of social experience and pedagogical operation which his clients may accept or reject.

The brief and tortured history of Risinghill Comprehensive School, Islington (1960–1965) illustrates in acute form many of the dilemmas of contemporary teachers which have been dealt with in this book. The high levels of teachers' role-conflict appear to have been closely related to the socially deprived character of the area[11] – as we would expect in the light of our research reported in Chapter Four. But the history of Risinghill is more than a sociological case-study; it high-lights the moral predicament in which teachers can be placed by their claim to freedom regarding educational means and ends within a system of compulsory education. Whatever sympathy one may feel for the headmaster's 'progressive' educational philosophy, his right to implement it in the context of compulsory state education is open to question. (The morality of Summerhill's 'progressive' position, on the other hand, is firmly based in the free and informed choices of clients for a particular form of educational experience out of a wide range of alternatives available to them.) Risinghill was the victim of the moral contradictions on which our educational system is built.

An educated democracy requires that the teacher shall be an expert in means rather than an arbiter of ends – which he is in fact within the broad framework of control maintained by the local authorities, whose elected members have virtually no say over the detailed provision of education, the curriculum of the schools and their extra-curricular activities. What is so remarkable is that a nation so self-righteous about its liberties should continue to tolerate at the very centre of its being the despotism of a self-styled *corps d'élite*, which decides the kind of creatures its children shall be, their life-style, their life-chances. Perhaps it is tolerated only because it is, in general, such a thoroughly unadventurous despotism, shaping nothing more outrageous than a standardized utility product.

The teacher in the maintained schools will cease to be above the morality of a true contractual relationship with his clients only when his monopoly is broken; this will happen when he and the school he serves are one alternative in a wide range between which parents can freely choose (after taking professional advice, and submitting to professional diagnosis, as they would if responsibly seeking professional service in any field of conduct).

The prerequisite of freedom is mobility. Schools at the secondary stage need extensive residential facilities (not necessarily boarding houses on the public school model, but hostels run by management committees of local parents, and approved lodgings in the neighbourhood). Different schools could offer different emphases, different specialisms, and in some cases an orientation towards particular vocations. Those which met no real need would go out of business or change their emphasis. There is no more fatal blow to English liberty than the area comprehensive school.

The answer to the contemporary problem of justice in English education is not to close the public schools but to make all schools public schools. To close them merely promotes equality of servitude. Their fees, of course, would be abolished, and they would come under the direction of local education authorities. But the local authorities would go into business, offering an educational service to the nation's children which would be sought after or rejected according to its merits. The problem of a central clearing house would be enormous but not insuperable. The system would be expensive; but we are now probably rich enough as a nation to afford social justice. At present we conduct our educational affairs like an impoverished nation which must carefully ration its allocation of superior educational facilities.

These measures would remove the teacher from his present position as an arbiter of individual destiny and place him in a proper contractual relationship with his clients. At the same time, while it would enhance the power of parents, it would also diminish their influence in directions in which it should be diminished. By depriving children of their parents during term-time, the boarding school equalizes parents; and it is the inequalities between parents – in their values, aspirations, concern and intellectual stimulation – which hitherto, as much as differences in inborn ability, have made nonsense of the pursuit of educational equality.

The teacher then usurps the parent with the parents' agreement towards ends which the parents approve: the morality of this course of action is the democratic morality of authority exercised with consent. Such provisions would involve the teacher in many duties which, in the maintained day schools at least he now tends to regard as not proper to a schoolmaster's task. It may be that he should be more generously helped by auxiliaries, that in the schools there should be new ancillary professions who help with the care and guidance of the young.

Wilson has argued that in modern society the teacher's role is necessarily diffuse;[12] Mays has argued that it ought to be. Particularly in the underprivileged areas of our large cities, says Mays, the teacher should also be in some measure a social worker.[13] He found in his investigations in Liverpool no marked inclination of teachers to assume this extended role. In our inquiries reported above (Chapter Five) the same reluctance to assume responsibility for social training also appeared. Rudd and Wiseman have found in their inquiries among teachers that the extension of the job to duties other than classroom teaching, to clerical work and school meals supervision, constituted a major source of grievance.[14]

It is possible that the employment of auxiliaries can solve some of these problems without impairing the effectiveness of teachers: too great and continuous personal involvement with their pupils over too wide an area of their lives can be as limiting and finally disastrous as a cavalier unconcern for pupils as persons. But it seems likely that the teacher of the future will need to be more *professional* if he is to provide an effective and democratic service for his clients. Like other professional men, he must be able to advise his clients, to provide them with evidence on which they can make reasonable decisions. (As he gets older – perhaps by the age of thirteen or fourteen – the pupil too must be regarded as a client, as well as his parents: he too has a right to choose what he will become and to select the services of those best fitted to help him to become it.)

The teacher of today and tomorrow is necessarily an assessor. The new Certificate of Secondary Education, which is designed principally for candidates in non-selective schools, who fall below the standard of attainment required for good G.C.E. results (spanning roughly the 80th to the 40th percentile of general ability), is to be placed firmly in the hands of practising teachers. They are engaged in all the technicalities of conducting a public examination and of carrying out research into examination methods; they serve on the council of the regional examinations board, on examinations committees, on subject panels and advisory groups. For

'Effective teacher control of syllabus content, examination papers and examining techniques is the rock on which the C.S.E. system will stand'.[15] This general policy is, of course, to concede to teachers their claim to be arbiters of educational ends; but it at least requires them to accept some of the responsibilities which this claim entails.

These developments, quite apart from more ideal considerations, require that the class teacher be an adequate educational technologist:

> For teachers, both challenge and opportunity (offered by the new examination) will involve a further extension of professional knowledge and experience beyond the confines of the classroom. They will be asked to enter a world which is in some respects unfamiliar – a world of examining techniques, calibration procedures, techniques for the validation of standards, research and development, and the like . . . the teachers must therefore equip themselves to understand means as well as ends, so that their control of the examination starts and remains sure and firm.[16]

It is extremely doubtful whether teachers are at present equipped to measure up to these new responsibilities and extension of their role; whether they are competent to qualify for the new freedom which is offered them. It is even more doubtful whether colleges of education are alive to the urgent need for a great army of highly competent educational technologists to man the school system in a manner appropriate to the modern world.

Whether he is providing a direct and routine service for his clients or assisting in the operation of public examinations, the teacher must be an expert technician. Philosophy is not enough. He must be skilled in the techniques of diagnosis, of evaluating the abilities and personalities of his pupils, and in prescribing educational procedures in the light of this diagnosis. And for this he must be equipped with the knowledge and experience of diagnostic techniques which enables him to provide reliable and relevant information.

But it is probably unrealistic to think that we can produce the all-purpose teacher who is skilled in the techniques of curriculum evaluation and development and at the same time powerful and effective as a class teacher. We need a new kind of specialization in teaching – between the front-line teachers whose personal relationships and mastery of their academic subjects are outstanding; and (comparatively) back-room boys whose main job is to evaluate educational practices. Teacher-training would take into account the special and different needs of these two kinds of practitioner. The distinction is not unlike that between solicitors and barristers in the practice of law.

The necessary qualities and characteristics of the front-line performer need more thorough investigation. If teachers in general are failing to make the personal impact on their pupils which is necessary if they are to achieve their objectives, the fault may lie in the muted teaching styles that teachers nowadays are encouraged to adopt. We need more research into the effectiveness of different teaching styles, and among these the 'charismatic' might prove especially interesting. We have stressed 'naturalness', even 'ordinariness', in the teacher-pupil relationship. It is not surprising that the educational consequences are ordinary. Effective teachers are probably extraordinary, larger than life, even theatrical, stylized: teaching is a performance, studied, deliberate. They have a touch of charisma (which properly directed training might enhance). And like most charismatics they can be difficult and distant in their personal relationships. Contemporary teacher training punishes or eliminates the charismatics. We have driven charisma from our schools. And we have failed to put even technical competence in its place. An alliance of unashamed charismatics and evaluators in our schools might provide clients with the effective service that they seek.

Appendix

The Provision of Private Education in the Nineteenth Century

The period 1820–1840 appears to have been a boom period for private schools. See E. L. Greenberg, *The Contribution Made by Private Academies in the First Half of the Nineteenth Century to Modern Curriculum Methods* (1953), unpub. M.A. thesis, University of London.

It is a difficult statistical exercise to compute the number of private (and joint-stock proprietary) schools in existence in the early nineteenth century, the number of pupils attending them and the proportion the latter constituted of 'middle-class' children. The Schools Inquiry Commission referred to 10,000 private secondary schools listed in an unofficial publication (see *Report*, 1868, Vol. I, p. 6); thirty years later the Bryce Commission quoted estimates of 10,000 to 15,000 schools with an average number of 40–50 pupils (see *Report of the Royal Commission on Secondary Education*, 1895, Vol. I, p. 51). This was thought to represent a decline since the eighteen-sixties. Much higher estimates were made by some contemporaries: 'Whittaker stated that there were 18,000 private schools in 1895, but would not answer letters asking for their authority for this statement. The number in attendance was put at 750,000 by witnesses before the Bryce Commission.' (See G. A. N. Lowndes, *The Silent Social Revolution*, 1937, p. 165.)

The foundation of middle-class schools for various religious groups was as follows:

Roman Catholic schools: Stonyhurst, the College of St. Cuthbert, Downside, Ampleforth and St. Edmund's had continental origins. New nineteenth-century foundations were: Mount St. Mary's (1842), Ratcliffe College (1844), the Oratory School (1859), and Beaumont (1861).

Anglican schools ('Woodard Schools'): Lancing (1848), Hurstpierpoint (1849), Ardingley (1858), Bloxham (1860), Denstone (1873), Taunton (1879), Ellesmere (1879), and Worksop (1895).

Quaker schools: Sidcot (1808), Wigton (1815), Bootham (1823), Mount School (1831), Leighton Park (1899).

Methodist schools: Woodhouse Grove (1812), Wesley College (1838), Dunheved College (1873), the Leys School (1874), Ashville College (1877), Truro College (1880), East Anglian School (1881), Wycliffe College (1882), Victoria College (1883), Rydal (1885), and Kent College (1886).

Primitive Methodist schools: Elmfield College (1864), Bourne College (1876).

Congregationalist schools: Mill Hill (1807), Taunton School (1874).

Notes

CHAPTER ONE

1. See *Report of the Schools Inquiry Commission* (1868), *3*, 45.
2. Ibid., *9*, 231.
3. Ibid., *1*, 308.
4. Ibid., *1*, 307.
5. Only 2·7 per cent of the Taunton Commission's sample of Oxford and Cambridge undergraduates came from private schools; but the latter provided 16·5 per cent of London University's students. Private schools more commonly prepared students for the Indian Civil Service, Woolwich, and direct entry into the professions.
6. Ibid., *7*, 64.
7. The Royal Commission on Secondary Education (the 'Bryce') gave similar testimony: 'The larger private schools, usually with boarders, are the private schools which do most for secondary education. They are often conducted on lines similar to those of the public schools; but they are less bound by tradition, and the larger scope for experiment which they afford has, there is reason to believe, contributed to noteworthy improvements of method' (Vol. I, p. 51).
8. *Report of the Schools Inquiry Commission* (1868), *7*, 66.
9. Ibid., *7*, 372.
10. Ibid., *1*, 291.
11. Ibid., *7*, 65.
12. Ibid., *1*, 645.
13. Ibid., *1*, 617.
14. Ibid., *1*, 645.
15. *Parents and Children* (4th edition 1907), p. 13.
16. There were also elementary schools with 'higher tops'—60 in London.
17. *Report of the Royal Commission on Secondary Education* (1895), *4*, Q. 16, 951.
18. Ibid., 219.
19. Ibid., 89.
20. Ibid., *3*, 46.

91

21. The London School Board's expenditure on science and art classes in higher grade schools was disallowed on the grounds that the school boards could provide only elementary education under existing laws.
22. Cf. BARON, G., 'Social Background to Teaching in the United States', *British Journal of Educational Studies* (1950), 4. 'The essential feature of teaching as an occupation in the United States, therefore, is that the teacher and the administrator are much less insulated from their clients than is the case in this country.'
23. BOURNE, GEORGE, *Change in the Village*, Duckworth, 1912 (1935 edition), p. 257.
24. For an interesting example of the Board of Education's cautious and tentative approach to curricular measures see *Report of the Consultative Committee on Practical Work in Secondary Schools* (1913): 'If a teacher is to do his best work, his individual bias must be allowed much freedom. We shall, therefore, confine ourselves to stating in broad outline the results of the experience of those best qualified to speak' (i.e. other teachers in elementary schools).
25. The Minister's duty is 'to secure the effective execution by local authorities, under his control and direction, of the national policy for providing a varied and comprehensive educational service in every area'.
26. Examinations Bulletin No. 1: *The Certificate of Secondary Education*, H.M.S.O., 1963, p. 3.
27. Ibid., p. 4. University teachers are, of course, still more extreme in their claim to autonomy.
28. The teacher's doubts about his role are similar to those Ralph Linton has described for many people in a rapidly changing social order. 'The individual thus finds himself frequently confronted by situations in which he is uncertain both of his own statuses and roles and those of others. He is not only compelled to make choices but also can feel no certainty that he has chosen correctly and that the reciprocal behaviour of others will be that which he anticipates on the basis of the statuses which he assumes that they occupy' (*Cultural Background of Personality*, 1947, p. 53).
29. CLARK, BURTON R., *The Open Door College*, New York: McGraw-Hill, 1960, pp. 148–152.
30. MANNHEIM, KARL, *Diagnosis of Our Time*, Routledge and Kegan Paul, 1943, p. 74.
31. See INHELDER, B., and PIAGET, J., *The Growth of Logical Thinking*, Routledge and Kegan Paul, 1958, and PIAGET, J., *The Moral Judgment of the Child*, Routledge and Kegan Paul, 1932.
32. RIESMAN, D., et al., *The Lonely Crowd*, Yale University Press, 1950.

33. FINLAYSON, D. S., and COHEN, L., 'The Teacher's Role. A Comparative Study of the Conceptions of College of Education Students and Headteachers', *British Journal of Educational Psychology* (1967), *37*, Pt. 1, and WISEMAN, S., and START, K. B., 'A Follow-up Study of Teachers Five Years after Completing their Training', *British Journal of Educational Psychology* (1965), *25*, Pt. 3.
34. ROBERTSON, J. D. C., 'An Analysis of the Views of Supervisors on the Attributes of Successful Graduate Student Teachers', *British Journal of Educational Psychology* (1957), *27*.
35. MUSGROVE, F., 'The Social Needs and Satisfactions of Some Young People', *British Journal of Educational Psychology* (1966), *36*, Pts. 1 and 2.
36. See WILSON, B. R., 'The Teacher's Role – A Sociological Analysis', *British Journal of Sociology* (1962), *13*.

CHAPTER TWO

1. KRATZ, H. E., 'Characteristics of the Teacher as Recognized by Children', *Pedagogic Seminar* (1896), *3*.
2. HOLLIS, A. W., *The Personal Relationship in Teaching* (1935), unpub. M.A. thesis, University of Birmingham.
3. MICHAEL, W. B., et al., 'Survey of Student Teacher Relationships', *Journal of Educational Research* (1951), *44*.
4. ALLEN, E. A., *Attitudes to School and Teachers in a Secondary Modern School* (1959), unpub. M.A. thesis, University of London.
5. COOPER, B., and FOY, M., 'Evaluating the Effectiveness of Lecturers', *Universities Quarterly* (1967), *21*.
6. GUMP, P. V., 'Environmental Guidance of the Classroom Behavioural System' in BIDDLE, B. J., and ELLENA, WILLIAM J., *Contemporary Research on Teacher Effectiveness*, New York: Holt, Rinehart and Winston, 1964.
7. MUSGROVE, F., 'The Social Needs and Satisfactions of Some Young People', *British Journal of Educational Psychology* (1966), *36*, Parts 1 and 2.
8. PECK, R. F., and HAVIGHURST, R. J., *The Psychology of Character Development*, New York: John Wiley, 1960, p. 190.
9. See ADELSON, J., 'The Teacher as Model' in SANFORD, N., *The American College*, New York: John Wiley, 1962.
10. WRIGHT, D. S., 'A Comparative Study of the Adolescent's Concepts of his Parents and Teachers', *Educational Review* (1962), *14*.
11. TAYLOR, PHILIP H., 'Children's Evaluation of the Characteristics of the Good Teacher', *British Journal of Educational Pshychology* (1962), *32*, Pt. 3.

12. The complete check-list was: old, young, married, single, has own children, has no children of his own, is like my father, is not like my father, man, woman, joins in, does not join in, is like my mother, is not like my mother, uses the cane, does not use the cane, fat, thin, gives little homework, gives a lot of homework.
13. Cf. ETZIONI, A., *A Comparative Analysis of Complex Organizations*, New York: Free Press of Glencoe, 1961, p. 181.

CHAPTER THREE

1. A Report of the Central Advisory Council for Education (England): *Children and their Primary Schools*, H.M.S.O., 1967, Chapter 4.
2. MUSGROVE, F., 'Parents' Expectations of the Junior School', *The Sociological Review* (1961), 9.
3. FRAZER, E., *Home Environment and the School*, London University Press, 1959, pp. 66–67.
4. DOUGLAS, J. W. B., and BLOMFIELD, J. M., *Children Under Five*, Allen and Unwin, 1958, p. 126.
5. Chi-square $= 0.09$ (applying Yates' correction) d.f. $= 1$.
6. Chi-square $= 0.14$ (applying Yates' correction) d.f. $= 1$.
7. Chi-square $= 14.5$ (applying Yates' correction) d.f. $= 1$. $p < 0.001$.
8. Chi-square $= 20$ d.f. $= 1$.
9. See FLOUD, J. E., et al., *Social Class and Educational Opportunity*, Heinemann, 1956. Eighty-two per cent of professional and business parents in south-west Hertfordshire (1952) and 87 per cent of parents in Middlesbrough (1953) desired a grammar-school education for their children; 48 per cent of skilled and 43 per cent of unskilled workers desired the grammar school in Hertfordshire, and 53 per cent and 48 per cent in Middlesbrough (see Table 9, p. 82).
10. e.g. DENNIS, N., HENRIQUES, F., and SLAUGHTER, C., *Coal Is Our Life*, Eyre and Spottiswoode, 1956. 'Parents are much more interested in the educational progress of their sons than of their daughters ... [but] for the boy who does not gain entrance to the grammar school at the age of 11, this interest ceases ...' (p. 239).
11. Chi-square $= 2.49$ $p < 0.15$.
12. Chi-square $= 2.09$ $p < 0.15$.
13. Chi-square $= 1.8$ $p < 0.2$ (applying Yates' correction).
14. Cf. DENNIS, HENRIQUES and SLAUGHTER, op. cit., p. 234: 'In fact, the bringing up of children is the job of mothers'.
15. Chi-square $= 15.9$. Cf. HALSEY, A., and GARDNER, L., 'Selection for Secondary Education and Achievement in Four Grammar Schools', *British Journal of Sociology* (1953), 4. Seventy-five point four per cent

of middle-class and 46·9 per cent of working-class boys claimed that parents had visited the school during the session.
16. Chi-square = 11·2 (applying Yates' correction) d.f. = 1.
17. The headmaster and staff have made strenuous efforts to open up all possible lines of communication with parents.
18. Chi-square = 26·05 $p < 0·001$.
19. Chi-square = 1·5. Cf. HALSEY and GARDNER, op. cit. No social-class difference was found in the satisfaction-dissatisfaction of parents with grammar-school boys' scholastic progress.
20. Cf. HUGHES, E. W., 'Children's Choices in Individual Activities in the Junior School', *British Journal of Educational Psychology* (1955), 25. Parents' interests as seen by junior school children varied with social and occupational background and were reflected in the children's choice of activities. Children in school A had mainly white-collar parents, in school B children had parents engaged in manufacturing industry as craftsmen or tradesmen. 'The predominant group of activities was often Art and Craft for both sexes. This was particularly true of the younger age-groups in school A, the Art and Craft giving way to Literature Pursuits in the older age-groups. School B showed the reverse tendency for Art and Craft to increase in the older age-groups.'

INTERVIEW SCHEDULE
(Excluding classificatory questions)

1. What is the name of the Head Teacher of your child's school?
2. What is the name of your child's Class Teacher?
3. Did you go along to the last Parents' Evening to meet your child's teacher?
4. (a) What kind of secondary school do you wish your child to go on to?
   (b) What are your reasons for this preference?
5. (a) Do you expect the school to guide your child in his (or her) behaviour as well as teach him school subjects?
   (b) If you do, what kinds of behaviour do you expect the school to encourage in your son?
   (c) What do you expect the school to encourage in your daughter?
6. Do you ever tell your child to help the teacher, do as he or she is told, etc.?
7. (a) Do you ever tell your child how to behave with other children?
   (b) If you do, what advice do you give?
   (c) Do you ever tell your child not to play with certain other children?

(d) If you do, what kinds of children do you tell him (or her) to avoid?
8. Do you think that too little attention is being given to reading, writing and arithmetic in the education of your child?
(a) Apart from the '3 Rs', which we have just dealt with, do you think some school subjects are neglected?
(b) (If the answer was Yes). What are these neglected subjects?
9. Do you think the teacher should 'stand over' children more and 'keep them at it'?
10. Do you pay for your child to be taught any skill or subject outside school?
11. In your opinion is your child doing very well at schoolwork, only fair, or badly?

CHAPTER FOUR

1. MUSGROVE, F., 'Teachers' Role Conflicts in the English Grammar and Secondary Modern School', *International Journal of Educational Sciences* (1967), *2*, and TAYLOR, PHILIP H., 'Teachers' Role Conflicts in Infant and Junior Schools', *International Journal of Educational Sciences* (1968).
2. WILSON, B. R., 'The Teacher's Role – A Sociological Analysis', *British Journal of Sociology* (1962), *13*.
3. MAYS, J. B., *Education and the Urban Child*, Liverpool University Press, 1962.
4. GROSS, NEAL, et al., *Explorations in Role Analysis*, New York: John Wiley, 1958, p. 18.
5. SARBIN, THEODORE R., 'Role Theory' in LINDZEY, GARDNER, *Handbook of Social Psychology*, Vol. I: Massachusetts: Addison-Wesley, 1954.
6. MERTON, R. K., 'Role-Set: Problems in Sociological Theory' *British Journal of Sociology* (1957), *8*.
7. LEVISON, D. J., 'Role, Personality and Social Structure in the Organizational Setting', *Journal of Abnormal and Social Psychology* (1959), *58*.
8. SARBIN, T. R., op. cit.
9. GROSS, NEAL, op. cit., pp. 274–280.
10. GETZELS, J. N., and GUBA, E. G., 'Role, Role Conflict and Effectiveness: An Empirical Study', *American Sociological Review* (1954), *19*.
11. MUSGROVE, F., 'Role Conflict in Adolescence', *British Journal of Educational Psychology* (1964), *34*.
12. KENDALL, M. G., *Rank Correlation Methods*, Griffin, 1948.

13. OSGOOD, C. E., et al., *The Measurement of Meaning*, University of Illinois Press, 1957.
14. Chi-square $= 8.06$ d.f. $= 2$ $P < 0.02$.
15. Chi-square $= 9.8$ $P < 0.01$.
16. Chi-square $= 5.6$ $P < 0.02$.
17. Chi-square $= 4.43$ $P < 0.05$.
18. Chi-square $= 12.80$ $P < 0.001$.
19. Chi-square $= 10.17$ $P < 0.01$.
20. Chi-square $= 4.92$ $P < 0.05$.
21. Chi-square $= 4.38$ $P < 0.05$.
22. RUDD, W. G. A., and WISEMAN, S., 'Sources of Dissatisfaction among a Group of Teachers', *British Journal of Educational Psychology* (1962), *32*.

CHAPTER FIVE

1. WALLER, WILLARD, *The Sociology of Teaching*, New York: John Wiley, 1965, p. 68.
2. BIDDLE, BRUCE J., *Role Conflicts of Teachers in the English-Speaking Community*: paper presented at the 40th Congress of the Australian and New Zealand Association for the Advancement of Science, Christchurch, New Zealand, January, 1968.
3. See MUSGROVE, F., and TAYLOR, PHILIP H., 'Teachers' and Parents' Conception of the Teachers' Role', *British Journal of Educational Psychology* (1965), *35*.
4. WILSON, B. R., 'The Teachers Role – A Sociological Analysis', *British Journal of Sociology* (1962), *13*.
5. MAYS, J. B., *Education and the Urban Child*, Liverpool University Press, 1962.
6. C.R. $= 3.7$ $P < 0.01$.
7. C.R. $= 3.6$ $P < 0.01$.
8. C.R. $= 2.47$ $P < 0.02$, 1.99 $P < 0.05$ and 2.35 $P < 0.02$ respectively.
9. C.R. $= 2.3$ $P < 0.02$.
10. Chi-square $= 7.03$ $P < 0.01$.
11. Chi-square $= 12.88$ $P < 0.001$.
12. Chi-square $= 9.31$ $P < 0.01$.
13. C.R. $= 3.1$ $P < 0.01$.

CHAPTER SIX

1. Role has been defined as 'the dynamic aspect of status'. See LINTON, RALPH, *The Cultural Background of Personality*, Routledge and Kegan Paul, 1947, p. 50.

Society and the Teacher's Role

2. A role is 'what the individual has to do in order to validate his occupation of the status': ibid., p. 50.
3. MALEWSKI, A., 'The Degree of Status Incongruence and Its Effects' in BENDIX, R., and LIPSET, S. M., *Class, Status and Power*, Routledge and Kegan Paul, 1967.
4. BEN-DAVID, J., 'Social Factors in the Origin of a New Science', *American Sociological Review* (1966), *31*.
5. For a useful discussion of these distinctions see MANNHEIM, KARL, and STEWART, W. A. C., *An Introduction to the Sociology of Education*, Routledge and Kegan Paul, 1962, pp. 12–18.
6. Sir Malcolm Knox quoted in *The Guardian* (22 July 1963), p. 4.
7. Chi-square $= 10.86 \, p < 0.001$.

CHAPTER SEVEN

1. The conjunction of ideas derived from Durkheim's sociology, cultural anthropology and Rousseau's political philosophy is perhaps best seen in Clarke's essay, 'Conflict of Philosophies', *Year Book of Education* (1936), Evans Bros. The authority of a 'culture' is seen as essentially like the authority of Rousseau's 'General Will': the child would readily accept it if he were fully enlightened. But by definition he is not fully enlightened; he must be forced to be free.
2. CLARKE, FRED, *Freedom in the Educative Society*, University of London Press, 1948, p. 13.
3. Ibid., p. 29.
4. CLARKE, FRED, 'Conflict of Philosophies', *Year Book of Education* (1936), Evans Bros.
5. Report of the Central Advisory Council for Education: *School and Life* (1947), p. 35.
6. *The Curriculum and the Community in Wales* (1952): Welsh Department Ministry of Education Pamphlet No. 6, p. 5.
7. WELDON, T. D., *States and Morals*, John Murray, 1946, p. 253.
8. BARON, G., 'Social Background to Teaching in the United States', *British Journal of Educational Studies* (1950), *4*.
9. Ibid. See also BARON, G., and TROPP, A., 'Teachers in England and America' in HALSEY, A. H., FLOUD, J., and ANDERSON, C. A., *Education, Economy and Society*, New York: The Free Press of Glencoe, 1961.
10. GETZELS, J. W., and GUBA, E. G., 'The Structure of Roles and Role Conflict in the Teaching Situation', *Journal of Educational Sociology* (1955), *29*.

11. See BERG, LEILA, *Risinghill: Death of a Comprehensive School*, Penguin Books, 1968.
12. WILSON, B., loc. cit.
13. MAYS, J. B., *Education and the Urban Child*, University of Liverpool Press, 1962, p. 105.
14. RUDD, W. G. A., and WISEMAN, S., 'Sources of Dissatisfaction among a Group of Teachers', *British Journal of Educational Psychology* (1962), *32*.
15. *The Certificate of Secondary Education Examinations Bulletin* No. 1, H.M.S.O., 1963, p. 3.
16. Ibid., p. 1.

Index

Allen, E. A., 17
Arnold, Matthew, 4
Arnold, Thomas, 2
Auxiliaries, employment of, 87

Behaviour training parents' expectations about, 31–6; behaviour to be encouraged, 34–5; behaviour with other children, 35–6; parents' claims to direct behaviour, 33–4; playmates to be avoided, 36; responsibility of school or house, 32
Ben-David, J., 71
Biddle, Bruce J., 58
Bourne, George, on sense of exclusion of country people, 7
Bryce Commission, 6
Butler Act (1944), 7

Certificate of Secondary Education (C.S.E.), 7–8, 87–8
Clark, Burton, 10–11
Clarke, Sir Fred, 81
Cockerton Judgment (1899), 6
Constraint and Variety in American Education (Riesman), 83
Contemporary teacher's role, 8–16; and local community, 9–10; influence of colleagues, 9; power and impotence of clients, 10–12; rejection of role as social selectors, 14–15; social realities and idealized view of teachers' function, 15; views of sociologists and psychologists, 12–13; views on importance of groups, 12–13; voluntariness, 10–11
Culture and Anarchy (Arnold), 4
Curriculum, parents' expectations of, 40–1

Dalton Plan, 13
Democracy in U.S.A. and Britain, 82–3
Dewey, 13
Differences of role conception and expectation, 59–63, 66, 87
Discipline, school, 50, 53–4; parents' attitude to, 39
Durkheim, 81, 82

Education Act 1870, 6
'Educational Priority Areas', 56
Eldon, Lord, 2
Examinations Bulletin No. 1, 8

Frazer, Elizabeth, 32

Grammar Schools Act 1840, 2

Gross, Neal, 45
Groups, views on importance of, 12–13

Head-teachers as source of conflict for teachers, 55
Hollis, A. W., 17
'House of Education', Ambleside, 6

Inter-role and intra-role conflict, 45

Kendall, M. G., 47
Kennedy, B. H., 2
Kratz, H. E., 17

Locke, John, 13

Mannheim, Karl, 13
Mason, Charlotte, 5–6
Mays, J. B., 44, 59, 87
Michael, W. B., 17

National Union of Elementary Teachers, 2

Open-Door College, The (Clark), 10–11
Osgood, C. E., sematic differential, 47

Parents: attempts to organize, 5–6; excluded from direct contact with children and schools, 11; impotence of, 11–12; influence and pressure, 4–6, 11–12

Parent's expectations, 64, 66–7; inquiry into, 28–42; area and class differences, 41–2; behaviour training, 31–6; curriculum, 40–1; nature of inquiry, 28–30; scholastic training, 36–9; separate interviewing of husbands and wives, 29; social status, 29–30, 33
Parents' National Educational Union, 6
Parents versus teachers, 58–67; inquiry into, 60–7; differences of role conception and expectation, 59–63, 66; nature of inquiry, 60–1; perceived or actual expectations of parents, 64, 66–7; restricted role conceptions, 62–3, 66; teachers' role conception, 63–4
Parent-Teacher Association movement, 11–12
Personal relationships, contemporary emphasis on, 27
Piaget, J., 13
Plowden Committee (Report), 28; and 'Educational Priority Areas', 56
Private and proprietary schools, 3–5, 90
Psychologists' views, 12–13
Pupils' expectations, 17–27; contemporary emphasis on 'good personal relationships', 27; 'identification', 19; older adolescent pupils, 17; research into, 17; teachers as models, 19; university students, 18;
    inquiry into, 20–7; children's and teachers' notions of a good teacher, 27; nature of inquiry, 20–3; results, 23–7

Rank and function, 76–8
Ranking and classification of jobs, 74–6
Restricted role conceptions, 62–3, 66
Revised Elementary Code, 2, 6
Riesman, David, 13, 83
Risinghill Comprehensive School, Islington, 85
Rousseau's 'General Will', 81
Rudd, W. G. A., 56, 87

Sarbin, Theodore R., and role-conflict, 45
Scholastic theory, parents' expectations about, 36–9; attitude to school discipline, 39; reasons for preferring grammar schools, 37–8; secondary school preferences, 37–9; visits to schools, 39
Schools Inquiry (Taunton) Commission, see Taunton Commission
Society and the teacher, 1–16
Sociology of Teaching, The (Waller), 27
Status and role problems of, 68–78; changes in nature and prestige of academic subjects, 70–1; connotations of inferiority, 74–8; education and training, 71–4; migration between different status areas, 68–9; rank and function, 76–8; ranking and classification of jobs, 74–6; status incongruence, 69–70; teachers' training colleges, 73; university departments of education, 75; vocational and liberal education, 72
'Subcultures', 80–2, 84

Taunton Commission (1868), 2–5; and parental influence, 4–5; maximum freedom for schoolmasters, minimum for parents, 5
Teacher, the, and society, 1–16; contemporary teacher's role, 8–16; higher grade schools, 6; parental influence and pressure, 4–6; proprietary and private schools, 3–5; rise of new despotism, 1–8; rule of teachers, 1–8; sovereignty of the law, 2–3; Taunton Commission, 2–5
Teachers and clients, 79–89; and C.S.E., 87–8; charaismatics and evaluations, 89; democracy in U.S.A. and Britain, 82–3; disregard of Community traditions and values, 83; employment of auxiliaries, 87; need for mobility, 86; need to make all schools public schools, 86; parents' rights, 83–4; private sector of education, 84; 'subcultures', 80–2, 84; teachers' claim to disregard clients, 79–80
Teachers' role conflicts, 43–57; areas and levels of conflict, 45–6; comparative study of four countries, 58–9; educational and social changes, 43–4; inter-role and intra-role conflict, 45; role-set, role-demands, role-conception and role-performance, 45, 47; U.S. research, 83;

inquiry into, 46–57; conflict and social context, 54–7; 'discipline' and 'personality', 50, 53–4; head-teachers as as sources of conflict, 55; in secondary schools, 48–50;

103

Teacher,—*continued*
nature of inquiry, 46–8; ranking of attributes, 47; sources of conflict, 50–4; working-class areas, 54, 56
Teacher training colleges, 73

University departments of education, 73

Visits to schools, parents', 39
Voluntariness, 10–11

Waller, Willard, 27, 58
Weldon, T. D., 82
Wilson, B. R., 14, 44, 87
Wiseman, S., 56, 87
Wright, D. S., 19–20